Understanding Teaching

EFFECTIVE BIBLICAL TEACHING

by

Gregory C. Carlson, Ph.D.

Evangelical Training Association

110 Bridge Street • Box 327

Wheaton, IL 60189-0327

Scripture quotations are from the New American Standard Bible, ©
The Lockman Foundation 1960, 1962, 1963, 1971, 1972, 1973, 1975,
1977. Used by permission.

7 6 5 4 3 2 1
3 2 1 0 9 8

ISBN: 0-910566-73-9

Contents

Preface

Understanding Teaching was first published in 1968. It was written by Dr. Kenneth O. Gangel, now Professor Emeritus of Christian Education of Dallas Theological Seminary and Director of the Graduate Studies Program at Toccoa Falls College. *Understanding Teaching* was added to the ETA *Classroom Series* courses as a replacement for *Teaching Techniques*, which was authored by Dr. Clarence H. Benson in the 1930s. Due to the popularity of *Teaching Techniques* (over 500,000 copies distributed), both courses were retained in the ETA curriculum, although the books covered much of the same ground. In the past 30 years thousands of teachers in hundreds of local churches have been trained with the help of this textbook. The dawn of a new century encouraged ETA to completely redesign and rewrite these two courses maintaining the core philosophy for a teaching ministry, with the added focus on training needs of twenty-first century Bible teachers.

This new revision of *Understanding Teaching*, written by Gregory C. Carlson, Ph.D. It is aptly subtitled, *Effective Biblical Teaching for the 21st Century*. Dr. Carlson lives in the Omaha, Nebraska area. He has served as professor of Christian Education at Grace University in Omaha since 1987, where he has also been Dean of Graduate Studies since 1996. He earned a B.A. degree from Grace University, a M.A. in Christian Education from the Talbot School of Theology/Biola University and the Ph.D. in Community and Human Resources from the University of Nebraska (Lincoln).

The new revision of *Teaching Techniques* is subtitled *Revitalizing Methodology for the 21st Century*. It will focus on the philosophical basis of methodology, insights from current research, an overview of classroom usage, and principles of selection for specific purposes and audiences. Designed as companion texts, both *Understanding Teaching* and *Teaching Techniques* expand the scope of previous editions and avoid redundancy. Together, they will help local churches more effectively train the next generation of Bible teachers to faithfully communicate God's Word.

Acknowledgments:

The author thanks Patrick A. Blewett, Ph.D., D.Min., Associate Professor of Christian Education and Dean of Grace College of Continuing Education. Pat is an administrator, master teacher, colleague, friend, and assisted on the chapters dealing with teaching methodology and materials.

Why Teach?

"And we proclaim Him, admonishing every man and teaching every man with all wisdom, that we may present every man complete in Christ." (Colossians 1:28)

"Why should I try to teach those kids?" That was the question asked by my Junior High leader after a long period of more discipline struggle than discipleship success. It is a good question. At a time when evangelical church attendance struggles to keep pace with population growth,[1] why should Bible teachers be motivated? What compels us to even attempt to bring understanding and application to our students?

Often teaching the Bible happens in less than ideal situations. Limited supplies, crowded or aging facilities, and lack of concern from the Christian community do not stop teaching. What makes Bible teachers satisfied with their ministry? Why do so many *love to teach*?

Whether you are a beginning or veteran teacher of the Bible, it really amounts to a question of encouragement. What is the motivation to teach God's Word to children, youth, or adults?

God at Work

Jesus was called "Rabbi" during His earthly ministry (John 1:38). This is a term used to refer to respected teachers and leaders. Jesus was a master teacher! Carl Shafer reminds us that because Jesus is our Savior and Lord, we want to pay attention to His teaching methods and activities.[2] Eldridge further emphasizes "we honor him as Lord and Teacher even as we look to him as a model of how we should teach."[3] Early in my career as a teacher, I turned in frustration to my partner. "Dwight, why are we doing this?" Half serious, he responded, "Because Jesus wants us to!" Since then, I have come to find this answer not only profound, but also motivating. We do teach the Bible to follow our Master's example.

In the Book of Acts, the disciples concerned themselves with *teaching*! The dynamic growth of the church during this time established teaching as a fundamental activity. Notice the role of teaching in the early church:

1. It was a mark of Jesus' ministry (1:1).
2. It was the means of promoting the growth of believers (2:42; 11:26).
3. It was a major method of evangelism, along with preaching (4:2; 5:25; 13:4; 17:16).
4. It was the missionary's qualification and occupation (13:1,2).
5. It was the menacing tool of false teachers (15:1,2; 21:21).
6. It was a mode of discipling the believers and developing leadership (18:24).
7. It was the motive of the Apostles (20:20; 28:31).

Christian teachers can reflect biblical examples. Our source of faith is also our guidebook for teaching! We teach the Bible to mirror the work God does through His Church.

Teaching, for the Christian Church, is not an optional activity! We are commanded by our Lord to teach! "Go therefore and make disciples of all nations,...*teaching them to observe* (italics mine) all that I commanded you" (Matt. 28:19,20). I do not believe Jesus put this statement out as a discussion item! It is a command. We have the authority, yes, even the responsibility to teach!

The gift of teaching (Rom. 12:7) implies another reason Christians teach the Bible. We have the wonderful opportunity to unwrap a gift, use it in obedience to the Lord, and build up His Body (Eph. 4:11-16). Unlike some birthday gifts we receive, God's gift of teaching grows in meaning and enthusiasm the more it is developed and used! The gift of teaching is the Holy Spirit's given and directed ability to impart God's truth so that believers understand how to obey. Unbelievers are also convicted through the clear application of truth. While many express their spiritual gifts through the role of teaching, motivational joy comes to the teacher who discovers and develops the spiritual gift of teaching. We teach the Bible because some are divinely gifted to do so.

God at Work in Our Students

Students live in need of God's help and blessing. Dismantled families, struggling churches, personal failure, and neglectful boredom have created a situation where many people do not even know God. Gather any group of Bible teachers together and they will share numerous concerns, challenges, and needs in the lives of their students. "Effective teaching is accomplished *through*—not *despite*—the needs and characteristics of our students."[4]

"We teach to see the lights come on!" So said a Bible college faculty member. Students have surprising insight and eagerness to obey God when exposed to His Word. "My goal as a Christian teacher is to provide situations in which learners intersect their thinking with the Lord, with Scripture and with other learners so that they might grow in the Lord."[5] When understanding occurs in a student, it is joyous! We teach the Bible because of our students' response.

Most any church service could be surveyed and reveal members who have experienced significant spiritual change through a small group Bible study or Sunday school class. This is not just a coincidence. As students apply the truth of Scripture, it begins to change their attitudes, values, even their associations. We teach the Bible because of lifechange in our students.

When students attend our classes over many months, we expect to see growth toward Christlikeness:

• Children come to know what behavioral standards are expected.

• Youth receive training to help them stand firm in their faith.

• Adults are exhorted and reproved in their walk with God.

The most exciting part of teaching is to see a thorough repentance and maturity begin to emerge. We teach to see our students obey the Lord and grow in Him. So often spiritual bonds form with those we teach. Jesus says, "A pupil is not above his teacher, but everyone, after he has been fully trained, will be like his teacher" (Luke 6:40). A depth of care and encouragement exists via the learning situation. We teach the Bible because of our students' relationship with us.

My teenage son returned home from midweek youth Bible study. He shared how he had learned to prepare and give lessons with his peers. In asking who the adult team leader was, I realized the cycle of spiritual generations came full circle. Who would have guessed that a wonderfully outspoken high school girl from 17 years ago would now be teaching her youth pastor's son the very principles she had learned! What a joy to see our students bearing fruit and producing results far beyond our initial expectations. We teach the Bible because of our students' future.

God at Work Through the Teaching-Learning Process

What do we mean when we say we are "teaching the Bible." A working definition is "one hand on the student, the other hand on the Word; bringing them together for life changing obedience." From this definition three assumptions are made:

1. We must study our students and discern their needs.
2. We must research the Scripture.
3. We must expect our students to change.

It is this third aspect with which we will most concern ourselves in this book. To undergird our work, let's examine the six aspects of the teaching-learning process.[6]

The *aim* of teaching the Bible is affirmed in Scripture: "But the goal of our instruction is love from a pure heart and a good conscience and a sincere faith" (1 Tim. 1:5). Who would not want to see these results in the lives of their students? We teach because we can know the Lord through the study of His Word!

A teacher once issued this friendly caution to an adult Sunday morning class, "You people are educated way beyond your obedience already!" This warned listeners of becoming engrossed in the *subject* for the subject's sake. What greater content is there to study? The love of study, subject, or continued learning each has intrinsic motivation. How much more valuable is it when we study the Scriptures? To see the entire process producing lifechange is a significance beyond remuneration! We teach the Bible for the sheer joy of hearing and obeying God's Word (Jer. 15:16).

Those who consistently teach have discovered the truth that to teach is to learn twice. How I view myself as a *teacher* enhances my motivation to teach. If I am a fellow learner, I conduct myself differently than one who views himself as a "fountain of knowledge." If I stop growing myself, I can hardly expect my students to be enthusiastic about change. Teachers need to view themselves as "professional learners, and our students as amateurs."[7] Teaching is hard work! It takes discipline. I remind my students, "All good teaching preparation eventually degenerates into hard work!" Paul reminds us, "Be diligent to present yourself approved to God as a workman who does not need to be ashamed, handling accurately the word of truth" (2 Tim. 2:15). Those with the gift of teaching are told to exercise that gift according to the proportion of their faith (Rom. 12:6,7). We teach the Bible because we have the stewardship of teaching.

A teacher's view of the student also impacts learning. Professor Howard Hendricks says "successful teaching not only opens the mind but also stirs the emotions, fires the imagination, galvanizes the will."[8] To have this effect upon students is the prayer of most teachers. We teach for the impact upon the *learner* (2 Tim. 2:2).

The environment of teaching is also a reason many teachers enjoy teaching. To motivate students with materials and methods designed to enhance their lives makes teaching worthwhile. Some teachers simply enjoy the challenge of establishing the best *learning environment* possible (see Chapter 10). We teach for the joy of establishing a learning situation.

When teachers compare what they are doing with what could be done, they find motivation to teach. The reward bench of Christ (2 Cor. 5:10) awaits those who assess their task appropriately. Parents want to know what is being taught to their children. Church leaders are concerned with effective curriculum. Our Lord is watching those who teach. We teach because of the eternal *evaluation* of our task. May we be faithful!

God at Work by the Power of the Holy Spirit

What sustains motivation for teaching? Reasons given by secular teachers certainly fall short. They often cite positive experience, contribution to the world, or the variety of a life in teaching.[9] Yet, the Holy Spirit must be involved in Bible teaching if we are to stay effective and meaningful.

Roy Zuck identifies three admonitions. The Holy Spirit illumines and motivates the learners. The Holy Spirit appropriates the Word of God as the core of a Christ-centered curriculum. The Holy Spirit empowers the teacher.[10] We can, and are commanded to, work with the Holy Spirit (John 16:13). Lebar and Plueddemann teach us that the Holy Spirit is the "only Teacher who is able to work both inside and outside the pupil,"[11] and we have a partnership with Him! The Holy Spirit is able to teach through us, and our cooperation with Him will keep us motivated. We have the power and authority to do so.

For Further Discussion

1. What factors diminish motivation in teaching?
2. Can you give examples of Jesus' teaching methods, attitudes, or techniques? Is it possible for a teacher today to imitate these same characteristics?
3. What evidence have you seen that God is at work in your teaching or the teaching of your church?
4. In what aspect of the teaching-learning process are you most interested?
5. What one step might the Holy Spirit want you to take to improve your teaching? Write down your personal motivations for teaching.

Notes

1. Ken Hemphill, *Revitalizing the Sunday Morning Dinosaur* (Nashville: Broadman and Holman Publishers, 1996) describes this trend, 18.
2. See Carl Shafer's series "Jesus: A Model for Teachers" in *Profile* (Wheaton: Evangelical Training Association, Fall 1994 and Winter 1995).
3. Daryl Eldridge, *The Teaching Ministry of the Church* (Nashville: Broadman and Holman Publishers, 1996), 22.
4. Klaus Issler and Ronald Habermas, *How We Learn: A Christian Teacher's Guide to Educational Psychology* (Grand Rapids: Baker Books, 1994), 55.
5. William R. Yount, *Created To Learn* (Nashville: Broadman and Holman Publishers, 1996), 95.
6. Howard Burgess, *Models of Religious Education: Theory and Practice in Historical and Contemporary Perspective* (Wheaton: Victor Books, 1996)

describes the six elements of a model of religious education: 1. aim, 2. subject matter, 3. teacher, 4. learner, 5. environment, and 6. evaluation, 21.

7.   Anita F. Woolfolk, *Educational Psychology*, 6th ed. (Needham Heights, MA: Allyn & Bacon, 1995), 10.

8.   Howard Hendricks, *Mastering Teaching*, with Roberta Hestenes and Earl Palmer (Portland: Multnomah Press, 1991), 71-72.

9.   Forrest W. Parkay and Beverly Hardcastle Stanford, *Becoming a Teacher*, 3rd ed. (Needham Heights, MA: Allyn & Bacon, 1995), 4-10.

10.   Roy B. Zuck, *The Holy Spirit in Your Teaching* (Wheaton: Victor Books, 1963), 93.

11.   Lois E. Lebar with James E. Plueddemann, *Education That is Christian* (Wheaton: Victor Books, 1989), 173.

Why Students Learn?

"And concerning you, my brethren, I myself also am convinced that you yourselves are full of goodness, filled with all knowledge, and able also to admonish one another." (Romans 15:14)

"Well, what do you expect?" We ask this question of friends, partners in marriage, or between teacher and student. Awareness and guidance of *expectations* are the keys to promoting interest and involvement of learners. Failure to do so results in frustration for the teacher and ineffectiveness in students.

Motivating the student to learn is the daunting task of the teacher. Must Christian teachers accomplish this task on their own? Has the Lord built in automatic learning helps? Do students naturally want to learn?

The basic premise for why students learn is that God created them that way! In the *Imago Dei* (image of God), present in all individuals, there is also an inherent tendency toward wanting to learn. "God has made us creatures of curiosity. We all have a strong, built-in desire to learn...Motivation to learn is an inherent characteristic of being human. Like any other, it must be developed to its fullest capacity."[1]

What supports this bold claim?

Foundational Factors

The Lord Jesus demonstrated learning motivation. This surprises us since He was God the Son. However, Luke 2:52 indicates that he *"kept increasing* (italics mine) in wisdom and stature, and in favor with God and man." Jesus grew in mental, physical, spiritual, and social areas. In His humanity, Jesus Christ "learned obedience" (Heb. 5:8). Students should want to learn to follow the example of our Lord.

Scripture records a variety of motivations to learn:

— Establishing the Passover as a perpetual event presumed the children would ask, "What does this rite mean to you?" (Exod. 12:26).

— When Hilkiah found the scroll during the repairs to the house of the Lord, the young king Josiah responded with appropriate eagerness (2 Kings 22:8, 23:1-3).
— The model and ministry of Ezra showed the same characteristic—"They asked Ezra the scribe to bring the book of the law of Moses which the Lord had given to Israel" (Neh. 8:1).
— "Thy words were found, and I ate them, and Thy words became for me a joy and the delight of my heart" (Jer. 15:16).
— Jesus said the children should be allowed to come to Him and that the disciples should follow a child's example (Matt. 18:1-6).
— The generational faithfulness of Timothy's family is commended (2 Tim. 1:5; 3:15).
— Paul warns the Ephesians not to be tossed about by winds of doctrine, but to grow up in Christlikeness via speaking the truth in love (Eph. 4:14,15).
— "Let the word of Christ richly dwell within you, with all wisdom teaching and admonishing one another" (Col. 3:16).

Students, when motivated, *want* to learn.

Discipleship demands a willing learner. Jesus never coerced his followers. He even asked, rather than demanded, if the closest disciples would stay when all others were going away (John 6:67). Peter emphasized motivation for freely giving to Ananias (Acts 5:4). Paul allowed his people to choose their own course of action (2 Tim. 4:9-11). Mentoring others for Christ involves working dynamically with people and the Holy Spirit.

Closely observing students shows they are always learning, but sometimes not what we expect! A student came out of a college professor's class and commented, "I learned a lot today, but not what he was teaching!" Students are consistently changing perspectives, reinforcing or rearranging thoughts, tracing their own intellectual side issues, looking for ways to overcome their boredom, or hungering for more. God created us with a natural capacity to learn and to grow. A teacher cannot *learn* for another person. Students learn because they are created for this activity.

Learning depends upon a student's willingness. Wesley Willis emphasizes that internal motivation is essential for effective teaching. He outlines three sources of motivation:

1. Need
2. Interest
3. Dynamic Interaction[2]

Employing one or more sources in teaching, learning is likely to occur. Students learn when we activate the proper sources of motivation.

Although God has placed within the student this natural learning curiosity, we must be careful to assert that sin disrupts and diminishes it. The unregenerate person cannot even accept or understand spiritual truth (1 Cor. 2:14). In the life of the believer, sin (both the condition and resultant act) exacts a toll upon the learning enterprise. Downs summarizes, "Because all people are made in God's image, they have dignity and worth. But Scripture and experience also teach us that human beings are sinful, failing to live up to the potential they have been given by God."[3] So, the teacher must be working in cooperation with the Holy Spirit to teach the Word of God. We do our part on the natural level. We ask God to do what only He can do supernaturally. "Christian educators are responsible to teach well and to pray well. They are in dynamic partnership with God, working in both the natural and the supernatural realms simultaneously."[4] Wilhoit and Dettoni explain:

"Christian developmentalists realize sin's pervasiveness and look for ways to overcome sin's effects on both the teacher and the learner. The Holy Spirit's power becomes crucial in the teaching-learning process as the sole means by which sin can be defeated and effective learning can occur."[5]

Developmental Factors

My nephew did not walk until age three. Prayer, medical care, and considerable effort were employed to strengthen his legs. Developmental issues became a concern when growth was not evident. Can growth in the spiritual realm be any less of a concern? Students want to learn because growth demands it.

When teaching students for spiritual growth, we must remember that age makes a profound impact. "The sources of interest vary with the ages of the learners, with the advancing stages of growth and intelligence."[6] Come with me on an educational inspection that evaluates developmental characteristics of different aged learners.

Meet Megan, age 4, as she is coming out of Sunday school. As she leaves for home, she might be heard saying, "I like being here!...Teacher likes me...I get to play...I can sing 'Jesus Loves Me'...What's in there?...My teacher says I am growing fast...God made everything...I am not as small as Mary...What is a 'offering'?...Are we going home now?...Where's daddy?...Is Jesus God?...Why don't you know my name?...You do it, I do it!...What are we going to do now?...Why can't I play with my friend?...Watch me, mommy!...I can do it...Feel this!...Why do we go to church?...Can I pray?...Why?...Why?..."

Sean, age 9, describes what he learned recently in Bible club. "Most of the time, I like church, I think the best part about it is we get to do a lot of things with our friends. Sometimes we get to go outside and play games. Then we have a Bible lesson. It's kind of like being with Jesus teaching on the mountain. One time I had to miss because my family had to go to my mom's work. But I read the chapter I missed. I read pretty good, I read 23 books last summer. I know about God, and I'm a Christian. We should talk about baptism, 'cause I don't know about that. God helps me do what is right! Girls aren't in our class. They're always saying they're smarter. We can memorize many verses. We're learning about sin and salvation now. Some guys think everything is funny. I try to get them to be serious. We get baseball cards if we memorize a whole chapter. Well, that's about it."

Charles discusses the people in his youth group: "Most of them don't get a lot out of church. Some go to meet girls. Or there's food! Personally, I like getting a chance to ask about stuff I don't get. And I like to be with friends. My mom really doesn't understand me, and since my dad left, well...I'm thinking about being a teacher. Or maybe a youth pastor. Maybe the world won't be the same, though! I'd like to help people work through worries about grades, their looks, and the future. I try to share with my friends at school about God. I use our interest in music to build a bridge. It's hard though, especially to the guys at my job. Work sometimes keeps me from youth group. But I'm looking forward to our missions trip. I'm hoping that God in people's lives will make a difference. It would be nice to see more adults going after it (walk with Christ). Well, see ya!"

Annie, mother of two teenagers, describes her church experience: "I don't think it's like it used to be! My mom always seemed to have us ready for church, devotions, missions conference, whatever! Seems like James and I live such hectic lives. Our kids are involved in so much school stuff and we both work. It is hard to make extra time for church stuff. We have found help during our tough time when James' dad passed away. It was helpful getting pre-marital counsel from our church. The young couples group we are in is great. I am involved in discipleship with Debbie, a young mom. The other day, she asked me how we kept our faith and marriage fresh. I'm not sure we do! I wanted to help her see that in the busyness of working with me for the 4s and 5s department, we also need to enjoy our kids' time now. The kids grow too fast! Well, I'm thankful for what worship at our church has meant to us."

By observing the developmental factors of these learners, we can assess these principles:

1. Age characteristics make a huge difference, even between youth and adult learners. To be effective teachers we need to know our students well.
2. Change is inevitable, growth is not. Application is important in every life situation (see Chapter 12).
3. Stressful forces of personal life, family, and society are always present. We must learn to cooperate, combine, conserve, counter, or sometimes conflict with these forces.
4. Knowledge, attitudes, and behaviors all become important when addressing the learner's needs.
5. We must study and utilize the best developmental information in providing a learning environment for our students.

Spiritual Factors

Micah 6:8 describes the requirements of God upon His people: "He has told you, O man, what is good; and what does the Lord require of you but to do justice, to love kindness, and to walk humbly with your God?" I see in this passage a behavioral dimension ("do justice"), an attitudinal dimension ("love kindness"), and a cognitive dimension ("walk humbly"). Our learners must have an encounter with the Lord Jesus Christ if any of these dimensions or domains are impacted.

Jesus compares the variety of learners to different kinds of soils (Matt. 13:3-9, 18-23). Some learners in our Bible study groups will be like the "roadway" learners. They harden, perhaps by the misunderstandings of life, so that the Word of God never has a chance to take root, and the evil one snatches our teaching away. Diagnosis and protection from the hurts, hindrances, and hardness of life is necessary for these students to grow in God (Hos. 10:12).

Other learners, "rocky soil," do not have the depth of life to do anything more than respond superficially. These students seem to always be willing to learn, but Christ is not making a difference. A deepening of spirit, coming from focused obedience to a few commands, may indeed be necessary.

"Thorny" learners (Matt. 13:7) are those choked by worry and wrong thinking about wealth. A spiritual battle rages for these students. They must train to cast their cares upon Christ. Weeding out the materialistic craving for things, stewardship of life should be cultivated.

However, some learners prove to be "good soil." They do not all respond to spiritual truth with the same intensity, but they produce the character of Christ in their everyday living. These students should be encouraged, cultivated, watered, matured, and replanted.

A student came back frustrated from his ministry assignment. He had prayed, prepared, and sought to minister to the needs of his club kids. Even though it was in what might be considered a "tough part of town," he was unsure of why there was no response on the part of his students. We discussed spiritual warfare and how maturity is hindered by "forces of darkness" (Eph. 6:12). He became much more alert and the Lord gave a measure of success in his teaching. Sometimes our students are hindered from learning spiritual truth because of the intensity of the battle.

So Where Do We Start?

Upon what basis do we begin to teach a lesson? Should we start with the Scriptures? The person? The needs of our church or society? Pazmino reflects on various approaches educators have used in the past, comparing the educational perspective to how one hosts a meal. "One host, the content-centered advocate, is primarily concerned with the detailed preparation and serving of the food itself and in making the elements of the menu consistent. Another host, the society-centered advocate, is primarily concerned with the choice of the food in relation to the group assembled. This host also considers the nutritional content of the food in terms of preparing the guests for the activities during and following the meal, and furthermore thinks about the ambience or context for sharing the meal. The third host, the person-centered advocate, desires to please each guest and is sensitive to the individual tastes of those invited."[7] It is the view of this author that we must integrate all three approaches. Starting with the Word of God (avoiding secularism), we assess the needs of students (avoiding boredom), to see Christ's work lived out in the home, church, and society (avoiding isolation). The most difficult aspect for teachers may be the constant mindfulness of our students' needs.

Let's Get Practical

We have doorways to our students' minds and hearts through "felt needs." Their perception of need shows their thinking, attitudes, and decisions. A wise teacher understands the root issues and utilizes the opportunity for application of God's Word. I normally maintain a "top ten list" of my students' needs. In that way, as I study the Scripture, themes that meet the most pressing student issues are more likely to be highlighted.

For Further Discussion

1. Describe the expectations your students may have for your Bible teaching. Are they different from your own?
2. What techniques might we as teachers follow from biblical examples in developing the needs of our students?
3. As you review the discussion of the developmental characteristics, what three similarities apply most to the students you are teaching?
4. How convinced are you that sound Bible teaching should start with a student's needs? Discuss.
5. List the top ten needs of your students.

Notes

1. Issler and Habermas, *How We Learn,* 103.
2. Wesley R. Willis, *Make Your Teaching Count* (Wheaton: Victor Books, 1985), 45-54.
3. Perry G. Downs, *Teaching for Spiritual Growth* (Grand Rapids: Zondervan Publishing House, 1994), 50.
4. Ibid., 55.
5. James C. Wilhoit and John M. Dettoni, *Nurture That Is Christian; Developmental Perspectives on Christian Education* (Wheaton: Victor Books, 1995), 38.
6. John Milton Gregory, *The Laws of Teaching* (Grand Rapids: Baker Book House, 1954, 1975), 46-47.
7. Robert W. Pazmino, *Principles and Practices of Christian Education* (Grand Rapids: Baker Books, 1992), 20-21.

Preparing Yourself in the Word

"And now I commend you to God and to the word of His grace, which is able to build you up and give you the inheritance among all those who are sanctified." (Acts 20:32)

"I don't know the Bible well enough to teach it!" Really? Many teachers with Bible college or seminary backgrounds feel the same. Yet, practicing Bible study and lesson preparation procedures will quickly ready you to teach the Word of God!

How well do you know your Bible? I have found the best way to grasp the message of the Bible is to teach it. Teaching disciplines me to handle the Scriptures properly.

Why start with the Bible? Because Christians are "people of the Book!" The Scriptures will change our lives and are the means God uses to build our relationship with Him (Rom. 10:17; Heb. 4:12; 1 Tim. 3:16,17). "Christianity is a religion of the book. God has chosen to communicate with people most explicitly in this book. God's people are expected to read and thus become intimately involved with God's revelation."[1]

Progression of Teaching the Bible

From God, through the text, to us. This could be the description of what the Lord has prepared for the Bible teacher and student. The Scriptures were "given by God" and "inspired" by Him (2 Tim. 3:16). What should we do with the text? What progression do we see developing in study and lesson preparation? Let us look at the approaches that would give us confidence in handling the Bible correctly.

Hindrances to using the Bible effectively in our teaching revolve around the study habits we form. We simply do not have the skills and attitudes to "handle accurately the word of truth" (2 Tim. 2:15). For example, some would say the Bible is boring! Yet, how is the most amazing book ever written, God's very revelation of Himself, and the perennial best seller, a boring book? "Truly the Bible is a miracle book! And from a practical standpoint the most wonderful thing about this is that God gave this miracle book to us for our own personal benefit."[2] We must have the proper personal attitudes if we are going to be able to teach the Bible well.

Misunderstanding the purpose and theme of the Bible creates a roadblock to effective teaching. The Scriptures were given to focus on Christ (Matt. 5:17; Luke 24:27,44; John 5:39; Heb. 10:7). The purpose, then, of studying and teaching the Bible is to shape the individual Christian into a Christlike image (Rom. 8:29; Eph. 1:9-11; Col. 1:15-22). Staying focused upon our relationship with the Lord Jesus will enable us to teach the Bible well.

Not knowing the message and content of the Bible hobbles some teachers. Nothing will replace ignorance of the Bible's message like studying it! A classic aid, used by many teachers through the years, is *What the Bible Is All About*[3] by Henrietta Mears. Wes Haystead's *Bible 101*[4] contains valuable helps. Many fine Bible handbooks are also available. A teacher or student must navigate the text of the Scriptures, finding its books, chapters, and even specific verses. Familiarity with the stories and doctrines of the Bible is critical. Knowledge and understanding of the different types of literature and basic theological themes in Scripture enable a Bible teacher to instruct with confidence.

The interpretation of the Bible (hermeneutics) need not be a hindrance to Bible teaching. Skeptics often say, "There are so many interpretations of the Bible. You can get it to say whatever you want!" I respond with two questions. First, have you read the Bible and studied it for yourself? Second, have you followed normal practices of interpretation, just like you would for any other important book? Answering these two questions usually eliminates most confusion about the interpretation of Scripture.

What are the basic principles of Bible interpretation? Kay Arthur suggests:

1. Remember that context rules.
2. Always seek the full counsel of the Word of God.
3. Remember that Scripture will never contradict Scripture.
4. Do not base your doctrine on an obscure passage of Scripture.
5. Interpret Scripture literally.
6. Look for the author's intended meaning of the passage.
7. Check your conclusions by using reliable commentaries.[5]

Following normal interpretation practices will enable the Bible teacher to progress well.

God has not left us alone to study and prepare Bible lessons. The Holy Spirit will illumine the Bible. This means that the Spirit will "lead us into truth" (John 16:13) and "bring to remembrance" (John 14:26) all things necessary to teach the Scriptures. We can depend upon this ministry.

We must also caution ourselves as teachers. The role of the Spirit is not an excuse for laziness. All the prayer in the world cannot substitute for a Bible dictionary. If we do not know the meaning of a biblical word, praying for the Spirit to help us understand the text when we do not want to study may border on blasphemy. Stein cautions us not to "use" the Spirit for our own needs.[6]

Biblical text and theology go together like cookies with chocolate chips. When one studies the passage of Scripture well, topics of doctrine emerge. R. C. Sproul's challenge is that "the issue for Christians is not whether we are going to be theologians but whether we are going to be good ones or bad ones."[7] A Bible teacher becomes a theologian when studying the nuggets of truth in the Scripture. These nuggets, then, can be refined and presented as valuable obedience in the life of the student.

The ultimate step of Bible study and teaching is that of application. Students must be led from studying the Scripture to obeying the Lord. Howard Hendricks frequently states "the Bible was not written to satisfy your curiosity; it was written to transform your life."[8] Chapter 12 of this book has specific insights for making the Bible live in students' hearts. This is the final and cumulative step in the progression of handling the Bible accurately.

Preparation to Teach the Bible

How does one start? Is there an expectation that one would be able to teach directly from the Bible? Effective Bible teaching can happen when a teacher moves through the preparation steps, then presents the lesson. What steps can a teacher take to move from the text of the Bible to seeing students obey the Lord?

The first step is to observe the Word. Bible teachers start by reading over a Bible passage or the verses which focus on a Bible topic. The purpose of this reading is to discover or gain knowledge from the passage. Teachers want to create, to the best of their ability, the mindset and intent of the original writer. We are looking for comprehension. As this reading occurs, questions form:

1. What key words, themes, or ideas emerge?
2. What is the mood of the passage? Its context?
3. What kind of literature is this?[9]
4. Ask "key questions": Who? What? When? Where? Why? How?
5. Ask questions of structure, e.g. comparisons, repetitions, illustrations, questions in the text, etc.[10]
6. Can you discern "observation cues" being used?[11]
7. Are things emphasized, repeated, related, dissimilar, or true to life?[12]

Once one has grasped the passage or topic, the teacher seeks to understand the Word. This step is often called *interpretation*. The purpose of interpretation is to clearly present the meaning of the author to students. One must keep the principles of interpretation (listed above) in mind as they describe what a passage means. Observation has allowed us to mine out building materials. Interpretation uses these materials to construct a place of learning and application for the student. These factors are essential elements of interpretation:

The Text—The words, sentences, and paragraphs of Scripture enable you to not only know what the author is saying, but to put the meaning into contemporary language. Many times I tell my students, "Scripture will interpret itself! Keep looking!" Our observation questions should have enabled us to get a grasp of the content of the passage.

Culture—Understanding the meaning involves taking a trip back to the world of the writer. Being a student of one's own culture significantly helps the Bible interpreter. The interaction between knowing Scripture and culture enables the teacher to sharpen meaning for the student. The more we know about the historical setting of the passage, the more we bridge to our own culture and period. All the while, we need to be evaluating our understanding with the pages of Scripture. "One cannot bring his study of culture to any kind of fruition without running that evaluation through a distinctly Biblical grid, an impossibility if he or she has too frail a familiarity with the Scripture."[13]

Integration—Psychologists tell us we all have patterns of thinking or schemas in our minds. When new information confronts our thinking, we must either ignore, adapt, reinforce, or extend those patterns. Our presuppositions, both theological and philosophical, must weld to the truth of Scripture. This creates the opportunity to intersect the present lives of our students, thereby establishing viable application.

Big Idea—The culmination of interpretation occurs when a central focus of a passage or topic's meaning is clear. Sound biblical preaching usually emphasizes a subject (or theme) and complements (or generalizes) Scripture. Effective teaching can do no less.

Wilhoit and Ryken summarize the criteria for a "big idea" as: "A good statement of topic and theme must provide a single focus for a passage, be brief enough to be manageable, be based on accurate analysis of the passage, cover the entire passage, and steer a middle course between undue generality and excessive specificity."[14]

When a teacher has the big idea, she can move on to developing aims (see Chapter 5) and then lesson plans (see Chapter 6). Succeeding chapters will delve into more depth on these topics.

The third step of Bible teaching preparation is applying the Word. It may seem strange to focus on application before the lesson is written, but one avoids a grave error in doing so. Too many times, Bible teachers do not bridge the gap between knowing the Scripture and obeying the Scripture. If we want to avoid "much ado about nothing" in our teaching, we must have intentional and specific application in mind before we write a lesson. Lessons do not apply themselves! The Lord uses His servant-teachers to guide students in living out the Scriptures. More about this follows in Chapter 12.

Let's Get Practical

The three-step technique described above to develop proper Bible study skills is called "flow question Bible studies." These studies prepare a Bible teacher to discover, understand, and then apply Bible truth.

Do you have adequate Bible study tools? Every year at Christmas, my father-in-law gives me tools. That way he has the right equipment for my wife's "fix-it" list. In the same way, Bible teachers need to collect the right study materials to excel in teaching preparation and presentation. Determine to update your personal study library, computer, or Internet resources.

For Further Discussion

1. What are some reasons people do not study and teach the Bible?
2. Trace the progression of understanding from text to obedience in your teaching. How does it compare to the Progression section above?
3. What are the three most important principles of Bible interpretation from the list above?
4. Which of the seven steps of observation seem to yield the most results of understanding for you?
5. Using the criteria for a "big idea," write a statement for each of these passages: (a) Matthew 25:1-13, (b) Psalm 23, (c) Jonah 1, (d) Ephesians 4:11-16.

Notes

1. Ted Ward in *Nurture That Is Christian* ed. by James C. Wilhoit and John M. Dettoni (Wheaton: Victor Books), 13.
2. Irving Jensen, *Enjoy Your Bible* (Wheaton: Harold Shaw Publishers, 1969, 1992), 15.
3. Henrietta Mears, *What the Bible Is All About*, revised (Ventura: Regal Books, 1997).
4. Wes Haystead, *Bible 101* (Cincinnati: Standard Publishing Company, 1996).
5. Kay Arthur, *How To Study Your Bible* (Eugene, OR: Harvest House Publishers, 1994), 60-66.

6. Robert H. Stein, *A Basic Guide to Interpreting the Bible: Playing By the Rules* (Grand Rapids: Baker Books, 1994), 70.

7. R. C. Sproul, *Knowing Scripture* (Downers Grove: InterVarsity Press, 1977), 22.

8. Howard Hendricks and William D. Hendricks, *Living by the Book* (Chicago: Moody Press, 1991), 284.

9. Jim Wilhoit and Leland Ryken, *Effective Bible Teaching* (Grand Rapids: Baker Book House, 1988), has an excellent chapter 11 which discusses the kind of literature in the Scriptures.

10. Hans Finzel, *Observe, Interpret, Apply: How to Study the Bible Inductively* (Wheaton: Victor Books, 1994), chapter 5 has an excellent discussion of the principles of structure.

11. Terry Powell, *You Can Lead a Bible Discussion Group!* (Sisters, OR: Multnomah Books, 1996), chapter 3.

12. Hendricks and Hendricks, *Living by the Book*, chapters 19-23.

13. Kenneth O. Gangel and Howard G. Hendricks, *The Christian Educator's Handbook on Teaching* (Wheaton: Victor Books, 1988), 76.

14. Wilhoit and Ryken, *Effective Bible Teaching*, 92.

Application and Learning

"Therefore everyone who hears these words of Mine, and acts upon them, may be compared to a wise man, who built his house upon the rock." (Matthew 7:24)

A young Russian public school teacher was asking my wife for another Bible. This surprised us because after Luba received her first Bible, she handed a stack of paper to her small group leader, and said, "Yesterday you gave me a Bible. Today, I give you my Bible! For two years, I have gone to a Bible study, and we only have one Bible, so we have copied our Bible for the week." Two days later she explained further, "My father took my Bible to his work, and everyone at the factory gets the Bible for one day. I won't have my Bible back for three months. May I have another Bible?" Two applications: One, do I study any of the many Bibles I have in my home like Luba studied her weekly scraps of paper? Two, am I as willing to tell the message of God's Word to my relatives and friends?

Perhaps this chapter does not seem to follow the one on "preparing yourself in the Word." Isn't *application* supposed to come at the end? This is partially true. If teachers do not plan goals and lessons with application in mind, they will not always achieve it. They may find themselves ending their class or study saying, "May the Lord add His blessing to the teaching of His Word!" I wonder if the Lord would respond, "No, you do it! I want to use you in applying My Word."

Evangelical teachers can err in application in two ways: They can pass on wrong or spurious applications not accurate to the text. Or, they avoid application completely, thinking it is not "real teaching" if there is application material in the lesson. We convey error when not "rightly dividing the Word of truth" (2 Tim. 2:15) or not dividing it at all! One pastor told Bruce Wilkinson, "I can't find anything to apply in my sermons!" Bruce responded, "Neither can your people!"[1] Jack Kuhatschek said, "We need to take the same care in applying the Bible as we do in interpreting the Bible. We need to be guided by sound principles of application, just as we are guided by sound principles of interpretation."² What are those principles?

The Goal of Application: What Should/Could Be

Chapter 3 examined handling the dual tasks of *observation* and *interpretation*. We now focus on *application*. The first principle has to do with the nature of application itself. Examine these statements carefully:

> "Application flows out of thorough observation and correct interpretation. Application begins with belief, which then results in doing."³

> "Application focuses the truth of God's Word to specific, life-related situations. It helps people understand what to do or how to use what they have learned."⁴

The entire process of studying God's Word, and then teaching it, is to produce a complete person of God (2 Tim. 3:17). This means going through the process makes a student complete; i.e., no part of belief is missing, faith is mature, abundance of godliness is obvious. Hence, this final step is called *application*.

"The goal of all Bible study is to apply the truth of Scripture to life."⁵ I sometimes tease my students when they give an answer related to application, "That is getting dangerously close to real life! Should we do that in academics?" Yes, we must push toward lifechange!

What does lifechange look like? The first and foundational step of application is to know our destination. We start the application process by grasping the *should* or *ought to be* of the Word. Our ultimate goal is to nurture Christlikeness; that is, being "conformed to the image of His Son" (Rom. 8:29). Conforming also means to leave the immature aspects of our new life, and grow toward a holy praxis (Heb. 6:1). This lifestyle looks very much like love. "But the goal of our instruction is love from a pure heart and a good conscience and a sincere faith" (1 Tim. 1:5).

Hopefully, the more seasoned we are as Bible students, the more knowledgeable we will become! The more knowledgeable we are, the greater our temptation to expound on the doctrinal and content areas, forgetting obedience is the measure of success. A Bible teacher must continually ask God for an applicator's heart. The study of Scripture poises us for obedience. Unfortunately, many sincere teachers think their task is done when they, or their students, are simply reminded of what *ought to be*.

The Context of Application: What Is/Has Been

Often, excellent teaching becomes like a dinner gone cold because it does not start where the student is. Students will be interested if they believe the learning will help them avoid a problem, enhance an area of interest, understand their own experience, strengthen and extend their values, and fulfill their goals. This is described as a person's *felt need.* "An educational need is something a person ought to learn...It is the gap between his present level of competencies and a higher level required for effective performance as defined by himself, his organization, or his society," says Malcolm Knowles.[6] I would also add the Lord, above all, sets the required performance standards.

How does a teacher assess needs as they pertain to application? Listed below are eight areas of personal application:

1. Relationships (family, friends, neighbors, coworkers, fellow believers)
2. Conflicts (in marriage, with children, at work, in the neighborhood)
3. Personal burdens (sickness, family pressures, death, loss, etc.)
4. Difficult situations (stress, debt, hindrances, etc.)
5. Character weaknesses (integrity, image, lust, selfishness, etc.)
6. Lack of resources (time, energy, money, materials, abilities, information)
7. Responsibilities (work demands, church programs, volunteer efforts, home projects, etc.)
8. Opportunities (learning, working, serving, etc.)[7]

Teachers know their students by looking at them through the grid above, comparing the evaluation with what *should be*, and proceeding to put forth principles that bring them together.

The wise teacher has in mind the specific application when developing their "big idea" and goals. Too many times, we do not ask the question "So what?" We only tell or teach "the what!" Before you are ready to prepare the lesson, the application should be firmly in mind.

Knowing the Word, knowing your students, and welding those together in a "big idea," prepares you for an application plan.

Plan for Application: What Can Be

Larry Richards states the pattern of guided self-application moves through four steps:

1. Generalization (of the principle from the text)
2. Varied Application (of the possible ways to apply the truth)
3. Examination of Sensitive Area (in the life of the pupils)
4. Personal Decision (what I call "cementing in the decision").[8]

Many teachers find this plan effective. The teacher reviews the big idea, looks for the relationship to daily life, fosters recognition of personal impact, and guides the response to trust the Lord for lifechange. This final response could take the form of an answer to one of these questions: Is there something I should...

Start doing?

Stop doing?

Strengthen doing?

Switch doing?

In other words, change is happening. Change can be evident when we see it in behavior. Or, change may bring insight to the student's thinking. Or, an attitude begins to emerge. Perhaps decisions are made. Spiritual fruit is being produced. God is at work producing lifechange.

We might ask, where and when is this change supposed to happen? Sometimes it will be during the class session. While not all lifechange will occur immediately with full observation, we can expect a significant portion of the Holy Spirit's work to happen right in the classroom before anyone goes away.

Perhaps most application happens after class. Effective lessons commence in real life. Your task is like:

– assembling a vehicle that will travel the distance in life!

– stocking the cupboard, so the cooking can begin!

– preparing the game plan, so the team wins!

– conditioning your athletes, so they win the race!

– nurturing the spiritual children, so they mature!

You get the point. Sometimes it is appropriate to intentionally plan a step of obedience before the next class. This produces accountability. It also builds momentum and celebration as the Lord works in class members.

The plans we make should usually foster ongoing growth. As a student obeys the Word, a fabric of godliness is woven. Over time, the discipleship steps clothe a life to cover a long journey. Stitch on with high quality and careful attention.

Are there any resources of accountability to help us in this application process? Who should we expect to maintain lines of responsibility and care? How do we "checkup" on our students? Students have six sources of accountability to use with variety and combination in teaching. Encourage students to be accountable to:

1. The Person of Christ (God)
2. The People of God (the Church)
3. Their Peers (friends)
4. Their Power Structure (authority)
5. Their Personal Life
     Their future; their conscience; their work and reputation
6. Posterity (succeeding generations)

As we plan for application through our teaching, we seek to provide the best possible environment for obedience in the lives of our students. The steps listed above help each class member take the "next step" of following Christ.

The Performance of Application: What Will Be

I'm motivated to apply, but how? Great question! Let me give you some practical helps.

Let's begin with prayer. "Application, therefore, begins on our knees. We must ask the Lord to reveal those areas of our lives that need to be transformed by His Word and His Spirit."[9] Ask your students to pray for and with you regarding the applications. Ask your friends. Pray by yourself, for yourself and your students.

We should warn ourselves that applications flow from Scripture. Too often we get ourselves in trouble when we try to be the source of lifechange, instead of allowing the Spirit to do His work through us. It is God's Word that changes lives, and we have the opportunity to see its impact.

Intentionally teaching for application is difficult for anyone struggling to personalize the passage. Some teachers shy away from this, feeling they are usurping the work of the Holy Spirit. Some teachers are hesitant because they lack experience, lack knowledge of their students, or perceive the student needs are too diverse. All these objections dwindle when we realize the Holy Spirit uses us to promote lifechange in our students.

Richards explains how to personalize an application: "It's looking over the broad range of possible applications of discovered truth, and focusing on those areas where it is most relevant to us."[10] When we personalize a principle, we look at the future and ask, "What would it look like if my students were obeying this?" Compassion for our students allows us to make our applications more meaningful. We seek to think what they think and feel what they feel—in other words, understand and make the truth personal.

I find that guiding a student to obedience not only involves a plan, it also involves persuasion! Barnabas' example should be followed: "Then when he had come and witnessed the grace of God, he rejoiced and began to encourage them all with resolute heart to remain true to the Lord" (Acts 11:23). We can model this by our own passion to obey and follow Jesus. We can ask them to develop their own plan, not just follow ours. We can ask students to choose how they will respond to the truth. We can ask each to tell someone else what they plan to do. All these ways assist the teacher in guiding the student toward specific application.

Let's Get Practical

First, note Howard Hendricks' nine questions leading to application:

1. Is there an example for me to follow?
2. Is there a sin to avoid?
3. Is there a promise to claim?
4. Is there a prayer to repeat?
5. Is there a command to obey?
6. Is there a condition to meet?
7. Is there a verse to memorize?
8. Is there an error to mark?
9. Is there a challenge to face?[11]

Second, my pastor during seminary days urged us to use Saul's responses on the Damascus road as our prayer for application: "Who art Thou, Lord?" and "What shall I do, Lord?" (Acts 22:8,10)

Third, one can also use the acrostic OATS as a helpful grid:

O = **Objective**	What is it I would like to see developed in my life?
A = **Activity**	What activity would create that life objective?
T = **Timetable**	When and where is this activity going to happen?
S = **Systematic Checkup**	How will I know if the activity is done?

Fourth, using the technique I call "cementing in the decision" can also be an effective tool. The details follow these guidelines:

1. What is my target?
   (What do I think God wants me to do?)
2. What is my time frame?
   (What is preventing this right now?)
3. Where is my team?
   (Who can help me with my decision?)
4. Who can I tell?
   (What one person will hold me accountable?)

Fifth, Thom and Joani Schultz suggest practical guidelines for change agents:

1. Cover less material more thoroughly.
2. Communicate what is more important.
3. Pursue understanding.
4. Ask good questions.
5. Allow think time.
6. Reduce reliance on memorization and lecture.
7. Use active learning.

8. Debrief all activities.
9. Help learners teach one another interactively.
10. Use a curriculum that works.
11. Sculpt sermons that result in authentic learning.[12]

For Further Discussion

1. Why do you think so many lessons and Bible studies are taught, but so little is obeyed by students?
2. Develop a profile of a student in your class. How should they look spiritually? Physically? Mentally? Socially? Emotionally?
3. If someone were to compare your students and your profile, what are the greatest differences? Similarities?
4. Apply two different colored highlight markers to a script of your last lesson, one for content (meaning) and the other for application (meaningfulness). What is the balance percentage? Is it fifty-fifty? Ninety-ten? Evaluate the implications for your students.
5. Are you developing an "applicator's heart?" How many techniques in the last section are effective for you?

Notes

1. Bruce H. Wilkinson, *The 7 Laws of the Learner* (Sisters, OR: Multnomah Press, 1992), 139.
2. Jack Kuhatschek, *Applying the Bible* (Grand Rapids: Zondervan Publishing Company, 1990), 10.
3. Arthur, *How To Study Your Bible*, 111.
4. Dave Veerman, *How to Apply the Bible* (Wheaton: Tyndale House Publishers, 1993), 15.
5. J. Robertson McQuilkin, *Understanding and Applying the Bible* (Chicago: Moody Press, 1983), 255.
6. Malcom S. Knowles, *The Modern Practice of Adult Education, From Pedagogy to Andragogy* (New York: Cambridge, 1980), 88.
7. Veerman, *How to Study Your Bible*, 144.
8. Lawrence O. Richards, *Creative Bible Teaching* (Chicago: Moody Press, 1970), 122-126.
9. Kuhatschek, *Applying the Bible*, 83.
10. Richards, *Creative Bible Teaching*, 162.
11. Hendricks and Hendricks, *Living by the Book*, 304-308.
12. Thom and Joani Schultz, *Why Nobody Learns Much of Anything at Church: And How to Fix it* (Loveland, CO: Group Publishing, 1993), 218-219.

Understanding Lesson Aims

"Therefore I run in such a way, as not without aim; I box in such a way, as not beating the air." (1 Corinthians 9:26,27)

The pick-up basketball game was intense. A professor had endured for most of the game. Almost a victory, all they needed was one more basket for glory and bragging rights! Whoosh! A superb pass underneath, an easy bucket. But wait! How could he have missed?

A determined teacher had persevered most of the year with a rowdy class of 5th and 6th grade boys. Yet, one lesson seemed to mean more than the others to the frustrated instructor. His lesson was well prepared, methods polished, discipline ready, then...nothing! "They just walk out the door as if they had never been here!"

Why no lifechange? It's a nagging question. Why do some Bible studies not "connect" even when we are seemingly well prepared? Could it be a failure to set goals? Whatever term you assign, your guidelines (aims, goals, objectives, purposes) shape a lesson, a class, and a life. The study within this book uses most of these words interchangeably, although other authors state helpful distinctions.

What is a goal? It is an action (behavior) the teacher wants to witness in the student's life. In *Teaching for Reconciliation* we read, "Teaching is an intentional activity. Teachers want students to learn. Every teaching situation involves explicit and implicit aims. An aim represents a value statement that prescribes what ought to be."[1] Leroy Ford further clarifies, "A learning goal is a broad statement of learning intent that expresses from the viewpoint of the learner the primary learning outcome."[2] With a specific goal in view, your direction for individual lessons, and broader spans of curriculum, are shaped, measured, planned, and used as a guide.

Value of Aims

Evaluation—The teacher is interested in goals because it gives him or her a basis for evaluation. It is hard to know if you are successful and effective, if there are no guidelines or standards. It gives the teacher the benefit of knowing when the task is done, or at least a measure of accomplishment.

Progression—Another benefit of using aims in teaching is to provide stepping stones for tracing where you have come from and where you want to go. You are not wandering aimlessly, but have a destination in mind.

Focus and flexibility—A goal-directed lesson focuses on specific needs and developmental qualities. Surprisingly, when specific goals are in place, it gives the opportunity for more flexibility, not less. The teacher's guidelines identify many methods that contribute to the desired response.

Confidence—Both teachers and students gain confidence when each clearly perceives what a lesson is about. One high school group caught on to their youth pastor's aims and took responsibility for the application. Later one youth explained why this unassuming man seemed to work so effectively with youth. The response was, "He knows where he wants us to go, and we're working on getting there together!"

Clarity and teamwork—Another teacher or helper more easily assumes responsibility when outcomes are clear. All team members are on the same page, working together, rather than individually. Perhaps you recall the illustration of a mother walking through the forest with her children. Spying a herd of skunks, she cried out, "Run, children!" So they all picked up a skunk and ran, but not too far!

Sources of Aims

How do you develop sound goals? Our mandate ultimately comes from the Scriptures. The Bible guides our thinking about what *should be* in the life of a student. Harold Burgess looks at the historical prototype of religious education and concludes: "In brief, the faithful were to have been inwardly converted through their response to the revealed message which had been received from apostolic times, and they were to live out its implications in the world."[3] Michael Lawson states: "Unlike other forms of education which stress content, command of the material, skill acquisition, and other data base requirements, Christian teaching includes the necessity of a change in living habits. We teach the Word of God not to satisfy curiosity, but to transform lives."[4]

What are these biblical purposes? It is hard to remember when you cannot get your students to pay attention! Experienced teachers work at refining the profile of an effective learner. Review the profile mentioned in earlier chapters. From our own understanding of what God would expect from a first grader, a youth, or an adult at their various life stages, we reset teaching/learning expectations. We might want to ask a series of questions.

Priorities—What are the key relationships and priorities in the life of the believer (John 17)? A person should have a centered relationship with God through Christ. The second priority of relationship should focus on other believers. The third should focus on building a ministry relationship with the world on Christ's behalf.[5]

Discipleship essentials—Jesus states three times certain actions would prove His followers to be disciples. Do my students have a regular intake, usage, and trust in the Word of God (John 8:31,32)? Do class members love one another (John 13:34,35)? Is "much fruit" evident in their lives (John 15:7,8)?

Developmental areas—Luke 2:52 models health in Christ's life with four areas: mental, physical, spiritual, and social. To look at our students in the same areas, with an emphasis upon the spiritual development, seems wise. The Christian educator is unique because he or she may be the only one interested in a student's spiritual development.

Emotional health—Is there emotional health in our class? I have rarely seen a growing disciple with an unhealthy mind.

Knowing God deeply—Are the students growing in their knowledge of God? Are they experiencing a walk of faith and obedience?

The above questions function as a lens through which we view students. It enables a teacher to compare *what is* with *what ought to be*. This comparison allows us to develop an understanding of the needs of our students. Then we can turn the need around to write lesson aims enabling our people to become all God wants them to be, one step at a time. In other words, goals are needs turned around from description to prescription. What was an area of lack, now becomes an area of intent and basis of instruction.

What biblical mandates has God laid upon your heart? We all have passages of Scripture and principles from the Word that elicit strong commitment from us. I often find the best teachers have spent time saturating themselves in the Scriptures, to allow clarity of God's purposes in their own goals, commitments, and lessons. Many teachers find it helpful to outline the general purposes they want to remember. These stated "biblical imperatives" serve as a navigation system (or North Star) for teaching. Wes Haystead outlines four such ministry goals for the Sunday school. They are practical statements of biblical mandates.

Ministry Goal #1: **Win People to Christ**
> The Sunday school must be committed to reaching people for Christ; those already part of a congregation and those yet unchurched.

Ministry Goal #2: **Teach God's Word**
A Sunday school must help people to both understand and apply the truths of God's Word.

Ministry Goal #3: **Build Supportive Relationships**
The Sunday school and other teaching ministries must be committed to helping build supportive Christian relationships between teachers and learners and among the learners in each group.

Ministry Goal #4: **Encourage Christian Service**
The Sunday school and other teaching ministries must be committed to leading people into active, intentional service to God and others.[6]

Purposes like these enable one to look at the state of the student and detect goals. Clear mandates discern the needs of students and serve as a source for helping us develop our goals.

Needs can be described as "performance discrepancies"[7] by those who state their intents with behavioral objectives. Pazmino notes that needs are also expressed in terms of the problem that exists, or the expressional objective expects a creative activity.[8] This book views a need as the disparity between where we are and where the Scriptures say we should be. Some of us are more aware of what should be. Our teachers are more cognizant of levels in student knowledge, attitude, and skill. In any case, the needs of pupils are sources of goals for our instruction.

Sometimes students are well aware of their needs. This is what teachers dream about! Instruction flows in a classroom that meets needs. Once a youth group, having recently experienced a friend who committed suicide, encountered a lesson on the subject of "Death, Salvation, and Second Chances." You can imagine the interest.

Conversely, most of us remember the other kind of dream (a nightmare) when students seem distant and are not interested in our lesson. This calls for the teacher to surface and stimulate the needs of the students. Fine examples of age-level needs have been published.[9] Chapter 2 also discussed some insights into this process.

Kinds of Aims

One confusing aspect to writing goals is understanding the many different kinds of aims. Some objectives will differ according to the time frame of their accomplishment. Curricular purposes are merely statements of intent, without many details of how to accomplish the intents. The further the goal is away from the present, the more difficult to be specific. Lesson aims are measurable, specific, and much more detailed. Units of study over a quarter or year do not have the same focus as an individual lesson.

Differences also exist when speaking of the role of the person setting the goal. A teacher matches instructional content to student need. The learner typically states how a change applies. A planner identifies the program's impact upon participants.

I once asked a class, "What does it mean for a high schooler to be 'spiritual?' What characteristics must we observe?" Ideas and thoughts listed included "that a person should not just know, but really understand." Attitudes were expressed, with varying levels of maturity. We identified certain skills on the board. Then, I gave this definition from Leypoldt: "Three kinds of changes are involved in making us new persons: Knowing, Feeling, Doing."[10]

I sought to express three spheres or domains of learning. Why are they important? Experienced teachers find that establishing goals in these three dimensions will enable sound learning. Rick Yount describes these domains as "instructional targets:"

Knowledge—Knowledge refers to the learners' ability to identify or recall information.

Understanding—Understanding refers to the learners' ability to explain, illustrate, or describe (in their own words) biblical concepts or principles they have studied. Learners who understand have moved beyond the actual words and grasped the meaning of the words.

Personal Response—Personal response refers to the learners' willingness to share a personal experience or opinion related to the topic being discussed. Values, priorities, and commitments develop out of the integration of truth and personal experience.

Purposeful Action—Purposeful action refers to the learners' ability to use what they have learned in class or during the week.[11]

Benjamin Bloom developed three domains, or taxonomies of learning, which parallel the description above. He labeled them *cognitive, affective, and psycho-motor.*[12] Many curriculum publishers follow this pattern. Around the world, you can find Sunday school teachers preparing their lessons around know, feel, and do aims. While not completely mirroring Bloom's taxonomies, they do mimic them. The following aims are found in current curriculums:

Knowledge Aims—The cognitive area involves what people think. Examples of this goal:

> Preschool: "Tell how Adam and Eve disobeyed God."
> Elementary: "Name a way God showed Elijah, a mother, and her son that He is powerful."
> Youth: "The club members will identify aspects of creation for which the psalmist praised God and depict these aspects in drawings."
> Adult: "In this lesson, you will contrast the blood of Jesus with the blood of bulls and goats."

Attitude Aims—The affective area deals with perspectives, or how a student feels, better described as the "attitude domain." Bible teaching often neglects this sphere. We simply struggle to implement instruction and training that achieves attitude change. I asked a veteran adult Sunday school leader the secret of effective Bible teaching. He emphatically stated,"You must know your goal! My goal is to comfort the afflicted, and to afflict the comforted!" Perhaps he knew how to set affective goals. Examples of attitude aims are:

> Preschool: "Demonstrate ways God helps him or her do what is right."
>
> Elementary: "The club members will grade themselves on how they reacted to parents' discipline recently."
>
> Youth: "Discuss ways Jr. Highers tend to be selfish."
>
> Adult: "Identify how you can remain faithful to God, and why you should."

Behavior Aims—Often the third domain is behavioral. In reality, all goals are behavioral because it is difficult to know someone's thinking or feelings unless it is demonstrated in behavior. However, this category is referring to the doing or skills ability of the student. Examples of this kind of goal are:

> Preschool: "Thank God for His help in doing what is right."
>
> Elementary: "Worship God because He is powerful."
>
> Youth: "Choose one or more areas of selfishness they will work to reduce."
>
> Adult: "That class members will be motivated to pray for their needs."

Response Aims—Larry Richards summarizes the above domains as "content aims, inspiration aims, and action aims." He describes another area as response aims. "When the teacher builds his lesson, he must think in terms of the learner response he hopes to achieve."[13] Often, more experienced teachers outline only one response aim for their lesson and blend the aspects of the other domains into that one goal. Examples of this kind of goal:

> Preschool: "To thank God for providing the food we need."
>
> Elementary: "That your students will plan ways to repay good to those who have wronged them."
>
> Youth: "Select one example of God's orderliness that will help him witness about his faith in God."
>
> Adult: "To encourage parents to share their knowledge and wisdom with their children."

Criticisms—The setting of goals causes some concerns. Pitfalls to avoid in setting goals are:

> 1. Going deeper (levels of maturity, intensity, and understanding).

2. Going broader (serendipitous outcomes excluded and narrowed focus).
3. Going longer (lasting beyond the classroom).
4. Going higher (more than jumping through hoops).
5. Measuring "on target" (not meeting the goal and missing the meaning).

Life goals—Some teachers have a "life verse." Others seem to have a "life message" developed over the course of teaching a class or leading a study. Some have listed their own "life goals" to guide their ministry and practice. Whatever format is chosen, God may be shaping the individual teacher with a unique set of learning aims and drives. Those who teach regularly without those overarching perspectives seem to lack passion when teaching.

Writing Aims

Four guidelines enable teachers to write goals or aims that are "brief enough to be remembered, clear enough to be written down, and specific enough to be attainable."[14]

Actor—The actor is the student. Goals should not be written for the church, the teacher, or even the Lord. We want to focus on the student as the one changing and growing.

Action—The action should be measurable or at least observable. Usually "action verbs" help in this area. "To explain" is better than "to understand," and "to define" is better than "to know."

Arrangements—Under what conditions or assumptions do we expect the behavior to occur? What knowledge, resources, and prior skills should be present to succeed at the task? These considerations involve what the teacher needs to provide for the student.

Analysis—What criteria will measure the action? Time, quality of performance, and other specifications cite how and when you would like the action completed.

Usually all four elements above are present in creating a good goal. More experienced teachers, however, sometimes assume certain parts and drop out key references to an otherwise sound goal in their descriptions. For example, instructors know the student who is the actor, or the arrangements are present, or elements of the analysis are understood. Wise teachers do not assume too much.

Let's Get Practical

Needs assessment—A critical factor of successful teaching is the ability to assess student needs. Too often we send a lesson satellite into orbit without proper communication systems aboard! Our "head is in the clouds" but our students just feel "overcast!" Bruce Wilkinson reviews the ministry of the apostles in the New Testament: "When they saw a need, that need set their agenda. They never came with an agenda and hoped it would meet a need. They realized that the most important first step of lesson preparation is the selection of the correct subject."[15] Excellent teaching firmly grips the Word, but also grasps the needs and growth areas of the student.

If a teacher keeps the student's needs in mind, it will not be difficult to achieve ownership of the goals. There will be a critical connection between the student and the Scriptures. The pupils will see how the Word of God can apply to their lives.

Often, teachers get concerned because they see so many needs in their class, they do not know where to start. They want to know how to have "something for everyone!" The Holy Spirit will help you focus on specific needs, and you will be surprised how broadly they apply. We want to offer specific principles (remember our "big idea?") without doing the work of the Holy Spirit. Look for clusters of needs, and try to think of ways your students will apply these principles. You will not have to shoot for the "lowest common denominator."

Shaping the lesson—In Chapter 7, we will look at how curriculums are properly used. One important principle in curriculum usage is to adjust or reshape the aims of each individual lesson to the students in your class or study. Remember, "an aim is a statement of what the teacher hopes to accomplish in a given lesson."[16] Who better than you, to know what a lesson should accomplish in the lives of your students?

For Further Discussion

1. What biblical purposes mean most to you and your teaching? Can you cite five or ten biblical references that support your understanding of biblical mandates?
2. Take an important Christian lifestyle concept like "holiness" or "peacefulness." What are the thinking, feeling, and skill dimensions of that concept?
3. Look at the aims stated in your church's curriculum. Can you classify them according to know, feel, do, or response aims? If you could rewrite them, what would you change?
4. What "life goals" do you have for your own life and ministry? How did you develop them? How could you pass them on to the next spiritual generation?
5. Practice writing instructional aims using the four guidelines. Have a fellow teacher evaluate your goals. What areas seem most difficult for you?

Notes

1. Ronald Habermas and Klaus Issler, *Teaching for Reconciliation* (Grand Rapids: Baker Book House, 1992), 137.
2. LeRoy Ford, *Design for Teaching and Training* (Nashville: Broadman Press, 1978), 31.
3. Burgess, *Models of Religious Education*, 62.
4. Michael S. Lawson, "Biblical Foundations for a Philosophy of Teaching," in *The Christian Educator's Handbook on Teaching*, edited by Kenneth O. Gangel and Howard G. Hendricks (Wheaton: Victor Books, 1988), 63.
5. Ray & Anne Ortlund, *Renewal* (Colorado Springs: NavPress, 1989), 10.
6. Wes Haystead, *The 21st Century Sunday School: Strategies for Today and Tomorrow* (Cincinnati: Standard Publishing Company, 1995), 19.
7. Robert F. Mager and Peter Pipe, *Analyzing Performance Problems or 'You Really Oughta Wanna'* (Belmont, CA: Fearon Pitman Publishers, Inc., 1970), 9.
8. Pazmino, *Principles and Practices of Christian Education*, describes these objectives, 100-101.
9. Charles A. Tidwell, *The Educational Ministry of a Church* (Nashville: Broadman and Holman, 1996), 235-260.
10. Martha M. Leypoldt, *Learning Is Change, Adult Education in the Church* (Valley Forge: Judson Press, 1971), 27.
11. Eldridge, *The Teaching Ministry of the Church*, 189.
12. Benjamin S. Bloom, et al., *Taxonomy of Educational Objectives. Handbook I: Cognitive Domain* (New York: David McKay, 1956).
13. Richards, *Creative Bible Teaching*, 102-103.
14. Findley B. Edge, *Teaching For Results* (Nashville: Broadman and Holman Publishers, 1995), 49-50.
15. Wilkinson, *The 7 Laws of the Learner*, 241.
16. Edge, *Teaching For Results*, 48.

Planning the Lesson

"I have many more things to say to you, but you cannot bear them now."
(John 16:12)

On the night before His crucifixion, Jesus had a specific, significant body of truth He wanted His disciples to gain. He did not simply tell them what they should know and expect them to sort it out for themselves. He had knowledge of the needs of His learners and a plan to communicate.

Contrast a contemporary teacher we will name Typical. He has studied well. He followed sound Bible study procedures. Keeping his students' needs in mind, he even created a "big idea." He wrote down the *know, feel,* and *do* aims. However, he now has "no idea" of how to actually teach his pupils, and class time is coming. It is not going to be a pretty sight! His ideas are reminiscent of a rainstorm, as lightning flashes of brilliance fragment his presentation. No consistent plan forms. Doubt clouds his enthusiasm, and he is flooded with misgivings about the impact his lesson will have. Typical needs a lesson plan.

Consider also the Carlson men, a dad and three sons, who spent considerable time gathering ingredients. They were creating a pizza *par excellant.* They turned on the oven, set out the bowls and pans—but what was the procedure? "What do you mean we need to read the recipe on the box?"

We may compare lesson planning to this process. How does one approach the specific lesson? Are there guidelines to follow that maximize the impact of Bible teaching? *Sunday School Standards* asserts a basic goal in relation to developing a teaching plan: "You have developed and implemented a teaching plan based on your teaching/learning philosophy, which provides for the effective sharing of God's Word with your students."[1] This chapter demonstrates the essential parts of an effective lesson plan.

Lesson Prerequisites (Raw Materials)

What are the ingredients of a lesson? When many teachers think about lesson preparation, they think of starting with the lesson activities, methods, techniques, and devices. However, the first part of this book has emphasized something different. Let's review. God's commission to teach motivates us to "produce the play" of Christlikeness in the life of a student. Students' characteristics and needs set the stage for the play. The Word of God is the script, and application auditions and assembles the actors. The aims of the lesson are like the director's touch. Let us look more closely at the individual parts of the teaching/learning process.

Prayer—Not only is prayer a part of the lesson writing process, it permeates all aspects of teaching. Prayer is communication with the Lord. In prayer we come to know the Father's will and find spiritual power and insight for the teaching process. Pray for your people. Pray with your people. Have your people pray for you.

Content—We start preparation by looking at the content or Scriptures. We want to achieve a mastery of that material. "We teach factual content, which is important because Christianity is a historical faith, not just a theoretical system or belief."[2] By thorough study and insightful contemplation, we achieve meaningful interpretation and contemporary application of the Scriptures.

Learner—We do not have a lesson without a learner. We base our lesson on the needs of the students in our class or Bible study. Sometimes teachers feel they should systematically move through Bible facts and principles, assuming the Word will sort out the needs of students. One would not continue to go to a doctor who does not discern the most pressing or life-threatening ailments and treat them first. Nor would we choose a surgeon who operated indiscriminately. We would also find it unacceptable to use a pharmacist who dispensed whatever medicine he had most in his inventory. No! Physical health demands regimens (systematic habits) and treatments (specific applications). Spiritual health should require even greater care and attention.

Aims—Focusing on what a teacher wants to say (big idea) and the desired responses (goals) are essential for effective teaching. We simply must encourage our teachers to state the central truth and select aims clearly. This pivotal step gives direction for what is to follow. It connects the Scriptures to everyday life.

Lesson—The task here is to develop a teaching plan. Using the preliminary work, fuse the objectives with the activities. This means a teacher must choose learning strategies suited to his or her class. A teacher begins to develop an approach to the lesson.

Evaluation—A teacher should be concerned with getting feedback in relation to the lesson. Chapter 11 develops a check list to assist in this important task. Without evaluation, a teacher can continue poor practices or stop teaching in effective ways because of lack of reinforcement.

Lesson Particulars

What should a lesson do for a teacher? If we know what a lesson's purpose is, then we begin to know how to plan one. The intent of a lesson is fourfold:

1. To guide the teacher in specifying educational purposes;
2. To outline educational experiences that achieve those purposes;
3. To organize those experiences; and
4. To evaluate whether those purposes have been accomplished by teaching the lessons.[3]

Ultimately, lesson planning should result in better teaching. Wilhoit and Ryken state: "We are convinced that the key to better Bible teaching lies at the planning/strategy level. In fact, many presentation problems (such as stating unclear ideas, being under stress, rushing through a lesson, or confusing a class) are the result of faulty planning."[4]

There are several particular types of instructional activities that we should incorporate into our lesson plans. Carefully crafting a lesson to impact students includes planning for these aspects in our teaching. Successful Bible teaching begins with the plan that we have. Bible teaching is more than just "showing up." Reiser and Dick summarize crucial lesson activities:

1. Motivating students.
2. Informing students of objectives.
3. Helping students recall prerequisites.
4. Presenting information and examples.
5. Providing practice and feedback.
6. Summarizing the lesson.[5]

Some would say that a plan or curriculum is unnecessary. Contentions include statements like, "We should just trust the Holy Spirit to teach through us," or "I depend on the relationship between teacher and pupil for sound teaching." Sometimes teachers feel restricted by writing down their plan. Unfortunately, some teachers do not have the time to prepare well or are lazy in their readiness to teach God's Word.

It is not that we want to bypass the Holy Spirit's ministry or the relationship with students, when we prepare lesson plans. We are not just creating limitations or unnecessary preparations when we write curriculum. We are working *with* the Holy Spirit, and in full relational potential, when we plan to use our classtime effectively.

Lesson Patterns (Curriculum Plan)

Robert Pazmino has identified different approaches to curriculum writing as emphasizing content, persons, or context. While philosophical understandings of writing curriculum are helpful, this section focuses on the practical writing of a lesson plan. Christian education publishing companies use a variety of approaches. We will examine three, giving examples of each. You will see similar components in all the models.

The first model outlines three steps. Briggs, Gustafson, and Tillman compare writing a lesson plan to writing a story. It must have a *beginning*, to prepare students for what is to come. The *middle* sequences the problem, the activities, and the solution of a lesson. The *end* signifies closure and is important to continued participation of the reader or student.[6] Standard Publishing asserts, "Readiness activities are planned to help students discover information they can share during the lesson." *The Standard Lesson Commentary* calls the three sections:

> Into the Lesson
> Into the Word
> Into Life[7]

Scripture Press curriculum describes each of these parts as:

> Focus: Tuning hearts to hear God's Word.
> Discover: Personal or group interaction with God's Word
> Respond: Applying God's Word to life.[8]

The Focus, or beginning of the lesson in this model, seeks to prepare the students to learn. The Discover section, or middle, seeks to provide experiences that enable learners to interpret and understand the Scriptures. The Respond section, or end, urges learners to evaluate, apply, and appropriate God's Word for their own lives.

A second model, involving a five-step plan, is outlined by Findley B. Edge. He sees a lesson following the pattern of:

1. Stating the aim.
2. Securing purposeful Bible study.
3. Developing the lesson.
4. Making the lesson personal.
5. Securing carry-over.[9]

Other lesson writers have benefited from a similar five-step process described in *Sunday School Standards* as:

> *Receiving Information*—There are two kinds of information learners receive in a Bible study as active participants. First, they receive instructions for what they are to do during the learning. Second, is information used to raise students' interest in the Bible content they will explore.
>
> *Exploring and Discovering*—(Notice the two steps are combined.) Active learners need to investigate on their own. This

leads students to discover Bible truths firsthand and learn they have personal access to the teaching power of the Holy Spirit.

Appropriating—Once learners have discovered a spiritual truth, the teacher will guide them into appropriating it for use in their daily lives.

Assuming Responsibility—Learners are assuming responsibility for the truths they have discovered when they begin to act on those truths and make specific changes in their lives.[10]

A third quite popular model of writing a lesson comes from Larry Richards—Hook, Book, Look, and Took.[11] We will use this model most extensively in this book. David C. Cook trains adult teachers to use these four components under the labels:

Life Need—When adults enter your class, they want to know how the day's lesson matters to them. Thus, in this step you grab your students' attention and prime them to begin examining the lesson's Bible passage.

Bible Learning—The heart of the Sunday school session is the time when you and your class members study God's Word.

Bible Application—After investigating the Scripture passage, you and your students are ready to consider how it applies to life today. Use practical information about applying the Scripture passage and pertinent discussion questions on the same topic.

Life Response—In the lesson's fourth step, use an activity or questions to help your students select a concrete way to put into practice what they have learned.[12]

Why spend so much time analyzing how Christian publishing companies write their lessons? First, because they are people who have much experience in helping people get into the Scriptures. We would do well to follow their example. Second, to help us use the curriculum that many churches purchase. Third, to help us realize that writing a good lesson is not that far out of reach!

Yet another perspective for developing a good lesson begins with an *attention* section. The activities seize the audience and direct the study toward God's Word. Yount warns, "Teachers make a dangerous assumption when they walk into a classroom thinking their students are ready to learn."[13] The attention part of your lesson plan enables you to collect your class, motivate them, and progress to Bible study. The lesson always begins where the student lives.

The lesson continues to the *acquisition* section. In this lesson part, the teacher is seeking to enable each person in the class to discover what the Bible says and what it means. The emphasis is upon facts, understanding, and accuracy.

The third lesson part, *application*, guides the students from knowing about the Word to seeing its implications. Drafting possible responses to the teaching of the Scripture is the concern of this section. Usually there will be a reiteration of the "big idea." Then a smorgasbord of possible obedience appears.

The final lesson section then takes the general implications and applies them to specific needs in the lives of students. *Accountability* secures a plan of specific application. Try to review the main points of the lesson, involve the learners in making a plan, and "cement in the decision," i.e., call for a specific accountability commitment. The result should be a personal, active response.

Once a beginning teacher heard me remind a class to "start with the Word." She dutifully outlined the "Bible Learning" section, had sound objectives, and had begun to put creative methods to the sections. However, she was still frustrated. "Do I write a lesson the same way I present it?" "No" was my response, "you prepare backwards from the way you present." In presentation you move from life (Attention) to Bible (Acquisition) to Bible application (Application) to life (Accountability). In preparation you start with the final impact and move to the contact section. Do not forget to do your homework—studying the passage and developing your aim—before you write your lesson.

Let's Get Practical

The hardest part of a lesson to write and present is probably the Attention section. While Chapter 8 helps you in selecting effective methods, Yelon's principles are very helpful for gaining attention.

Seventeen Techniques to Make Meaningful Attention-Getters

1. Relate whatever is taught to a strong student interest.
2. Provide a real problem to start the unit.
3. Provide a simulated role within a real situation.
4. State the connection—where and when the content is used.
5. State or show the use and its payoff.
6. Use a meaningful quotation.
7. Use a meaningful generalization.
8. Tell of successful application.
9. Tell of likely problems if the ideas are not applied or understood.
10. Conduct an activity demonstrating need.
11. Ask a puzzling relevant question to show the content is needed.
12. Show a relevant puzzling event.
13. Ask which relevant idea is correct.
14. Present an unsolved case.

15. Contrast students' beliefs and students' actions with their self-view.
16. Ask students why they think the topic is important.
17. Give a case or an activity and ask students how the topic is relevant for them.[14]

For Further Discussion

1. Did Jesus use a "plan" when He taught? What evidence can you give for your answer?
2. Review the prerequisites for a specific lesson. What ingredient is most often left out of your teaching preparation?
3. What benefits have you discovered from planning a Bible lesson or class? Are there any detriments to planning a lesson?
4. Compare the three models of lesson plans. What parts are similar? Different?
5. Choose one "attention-getter" and refine it for use in a lesson that you are soon to teach.

Notes

1. Lowell E. Brown, *Sunday School Standards* (Ventura, CA: Gospel Light Publications, 1986), 27.
2. Kevin E. Lawson, "Effective Teaching: Implications from Current Research," *Christian Education Journal*, Vol. XI, No. 3 (Wheaton: Scripture Press Ministries, Spring 1991), 54.
3. Ralph Tyler, *Basic Principles of Curriculum and Instruction* (Chicago: University of Chicago Press, 1949).
4. Leland Ryken and James Wilhoit, "Teaching the Bible: The Church's Unfinished Task," *Christian Education Journal*, Vol. X, No. 2 (Wheaton: Scripture Press Ministries, Winter 1990), 43.
5. Robert A. Reiser and Walter Dick, *Instructional Planning, A Guide for Teachers*, 2nd ed. (Boston: Allyn and Bacon, 1996), 47-51.
6. Leslie J. Briggs, Kent L. Gustafson, and Murray H. Tillman, eds., *Instructional Design Principles and Applications*, 2nd ed. (Englewood Cliffs, NJ: Educational Technology Publications, 1991), 179-181.
7. Standard Publishing, Patricia Alderdice Senseman, ed. *Christians in Action*, Middler Curriculum (Cincinnati: Standard Publishing Company, Summer 1997), 2.
8. Scripture Press Teaching Guide, *Studies in Ecclesiastes and Song of Songs* (Colorado Springs: Scripture Press, June, July, August 1997).
9. Edge, *Teaching for Results*, 106.
10. Brown, *Sunday School Standards*, 19-20.
11. Richards, *Creative Bible Teaching*, 108-114.
12. Dan Lioy, ed., Adult Teacher's Guide, *David C. Cook's Bible in Life Curriculum* (Colorado Springs: Cook Communications, June, July, August 1997), 5.

13. Rick Yount, "Planning to Teach" in *The Teaching Ministry of the Church* (Nashville: Broadman & Holman, 1995), 190.
14. Stephen L. Yelon, *Powerful Principles of Instruction* (White Plains, NY: Longman Publishing, 1996), 281.

Teaching Students–
Not Lessons

"Oh, how I love your law, I meditate on it all day long." (Psalm 119:97)

Whenever I sit in a Christian Education committee meeting, it is only a matter of time before I hear complaints about curriculum. Committee members grumble because teachers do not feel successful. Since the committee knows the teachers are good people, they conclude the problem must be with the curriculum materials. The amazing thing about this scenario is the fact that it makes little difference which publisher is in question.

Conversely, when I consult with major curriculum publishers, I find faithful, competent writers, editors, artists, and educators producing materials that teach the Bible in an age-appropriate, active learning format. Most workers at publishing houses are active teachers themselves. They are constantly using their materials to make sure it can be effective in the classroom. So why is there so much criticism about curriculum?

Perhaps the primary source of teacher frustration is the fact that many teachers never learn how to use the curriculum designated for their particular classes. This chapter will focus on how teachers should use curriculum materials. As we think about curriculum, some basic principles will help us become more effective teachers.

What Is Curriculum?

Curriculum, simply defined, is a course of study. It implies a teacher has an organized plan for the teaching time. Using curriculum implies the teacher knows what to accomplish. It also implies the content to learn is in some type of sequence. For example, think of a mathematics curriculum for first grade through high school. It is understood that someone has sequenced the learning of math so that elementary principles, like addition and subtraction, are learned before students attempt multiplication and division. A solid knowledge of basic mathematics is necessary before the student can learn principles of algebra or calculus.

In the same way, Bible information is organized to address elementary concepts before ideas of depth. This mastery of Bible concepts is a curriculum. In one sense, this is precisely what the pastor does each week as he prepares a sequence of sermons to help a congregation grow.

If time, knowledge, resources, training, and confidence exist, teachers can organize a curriculum or course of study on their own. Teachers can decide what lifechange to incorporate into the lesson. The truths of God's Word that stimulate students toward the defined outcome can be explored. Teachers can also prepare learning activities that help their students interact with the Word. With access to desktop publishing, a teacher can design and print appropriate worksheets, art projects, or games to enhance the learning process. While writing one's own curriculum sounds like it would be fun, it also sounds like enormous work, especially week after week!

Most teachers do not have the criteria to create new curriculum each week. Even among teachers who have everything they need to prepare their own curriculum, the quality of their product appears limited. Compared to purchased materials, there is no setting to test and refine the items. When teachers have the desire, ability, and resources to produce quality materials, churches should allow them to exercise their wonderful gifts and share them with a variety of churches. The classic story of such a gifted teacher was Henrietta Mears.

Since the invention of the printing press, churches and gifted teachers have worked together in preparing and sharing materials. Books were one of the first forms of printed curriculum. Over the past two hundred years, organizations have formed with the vision of helping Bible teachers effectively teach and share the gospel with children. As these publishing ministries grew, churches found it cost-effective to purchase products to help their teachers systematically teach the Bible. Particularly for Sunday school programs, these materials included age-appropriate learning activities, pictures, and take-home papers to reinforce the Bible lesson. With the arrival of club programs, curriculum began including handbooks, game times, and group meetings. Present and future curriculum takes the form of CD-ROMs, computer games, and Internet learning links and "chat rooms."

It is important to note publishers categorize curriculum differently. One category, called *uniform curriculum,* is defined as a course of study using the same text for all students. In other words, every student (regardless of age) studies the same lesson at an age-appropriate level.

A second category, called *departmentally graded curriculum,* defines curriculum as a course of study arranged so that all students within the same department study the same lesson. This structure allows different age levels to study different topics. It emphasizes Bible stories being taught at age-appropriate levels, and also age-appropriate life application. One of its strengths is its flexibility for different size churches.

The third category of curriculum is called *closely graded curriculum* and involves a course of study for use with students in classes or departments. This structure is based on specific grade levels in public school or closely associated ages. It emphasizes the common characteristics of the age level to provide appropriate life application to a relevant Bible lesson. Lessons are selected because of their appropriateness to meeting age-related needs. These concepts are understood best as one comprehends the idea of a *scope and sequence.*

Another type of curriculum used is *catechism.* This format asks questions and provides appropriate responses for students to learn and often recite.

A final category, especially popular in youth and adult divisions, is the *elective* method. The format offers study topics based on current student or teacher interests, as opposed to following a scope and sequence for systematic study.

What Is a Scope and Sequence?

A *scope and sequence* design is simply a matrix defining (1) *what content will be taught* (the scope of study) and (2) *in what order the material will be presented* (the sequence of study). Every publisher has a defined scope and sequence for its curriculum. From the scope and sequence, all writers, editors, artists, and educators design the material.

What Is the Publisher's Foundation?

While a publisher's scope and sequence provides the road map for its curriculum, it is important to understand two other guiding documents your publisher uses to produce its materials. One of those documents is the publisher's philosophy of education. The other document is the publisher's doctrinal statement.

The publisher's philosophy of education is a brief document that describes what the publisher believes teaching and learning should look like in classrooms using its materials. This document may define its curriculum as either uniform, departmentally graded, closely graded, catechism, or elective study. This document helps your publisher define and organize the typical learning process within a classroom.

A publisher's doctrinal statement is the eye into its soul. From this document, we determine the publisher's view on inspiration of Scripture, the person and work of Jesus Christ, salvation, and other doctrines significant to your church. Sometimes, a publisher's doctrinal statement reveals either a lack of doctrinal clarity or broader worldview than your church. As teachers, our task determines appropriate inclusion of doctrinal differences.

To fully understand what a publisher believes a teacher should accomplish, evaluate the publisher's philosophy of education statement and doctrinal statement along with its scope and sequence. A reputable publisher makes these documents available upon request.

Most publishers rest on the stability of God's Word to provide answers to life's questions. Publishers also want to package God's truth in a way that is attractive and contemporary to its students.

Let's Get Practical

Teachers can understand the purpose and use of curriculum by keeping their focus on students, not curriculum materials. Listed below are some practical tips to enhance usage of your curriculum:

1. Spend time meditating on God's Word, praying specifically for each of your students.
2. Focus on the objectives for each lesson.
3. View the Bible as your curriculum.
4. Do what is best for class fellowship, interaction, worship and prayer.
5. Choose learning activities that fit your class.
6. Organize all the supplies you need before class.

The principle is this—*the teacher controls the curriculum, not vice versa!* God holds the teacher accountable for the class experience, not the printed material.

For Further Discussion

1. What is the philosophy of education for your curriculum publisher?
2. What were the Bible knowledge and life application objectives of last Sunday's Sunday school lesson?
3. The key verse for this chapter is from Psalm 119. How did the writer of that psalm organize his course of study so that students could remember the outline as he taught about the beauty and value of God's Word? (Hint: Do you know the Hebrew alphabet?)
4. How can you organize your weekly routine so that you have adequate preparation for your lesson before you arrive at the church?
5. Following is a list of curriculum publishers and their addresses. Contact two ro three publishers to review their philosophy of education statement, doctrinal statement, and scope and sequence? If, per chance, your publisher is not listed below, find its address in your teacher's guide.

Curriculum Publishers

Abington Press/Cokesbury
201 Eighth Ave. S
Nashville, TN 37202

Accent Publications
7125 Bisc Dr.
Colorado Springs, CO 80918

Augsburg Fortress Publishers
426 S. Fifth St.
PO Box 1209
Minneapolis, MN 55440

CRC Publications
2850 Kalamazoo Ave. SE
Grand Rapids, MI 49560

CharismaLife
600 Rinehart Rd.
Lake Mary, FL 32746

Christian Board of Publications/
  Chalice Press
1316 Convention Plaza Dr.
PO Box 179
St. Louis, MO 63166-0179

Concordia Publishing House
3558 S. Jefferson Ave.
St. Louis, MO 63118

David C. Cook Publishing
4050 Lee Vance View
Colorado Springs, CO 80918

Echoes
  Div. of Cook Church Ministries
4050 Lee Vance View
Colorado Springs, CO 80918

Faith & Fellowship Press
704 W. Vernon Ave.
Fergus Falls, MN 56538-0655

Faith & Life Press
PO Box 347
Newton, KS 67114-0347

Gospel Light Publishing
2300 Knoll Ave.
Ventura, CA 93003

Group Publishing
1515 Cascade Ave.
Loveland, CO 80538

Judson Press
PO Box 851
Valley Forge, PA 19482

National Baptist Publishing
6717 Centennial Blvd.
Nashville, TN 37209

Pathway Press
1080 Montgomery Ave.
Cleveland, TN 37311

Pentecostal Publishing House
8855 Dunn Rd.
Hazelwood, MO 63042

Radiant Life Publishing
1445 Boonville Ave.
Springfield, MO 65804

Randall House Publications
PO Box 17306
Nashville, TN 37217

Curriculum Publishers (con't.)

Scripture Press
4050 Lee Vance View
Colorado Springs, CO 80918

Standard Publishing
8121 Hamilton Ave.
Cincinnati, OH 45231

The Sunday School Board
  of the Southern Baptist Conv.
127 Ninth Ave. N.
Nashville, TN 37234

Treasure Publishing
  (formerly Roper Press)
829 S. Shields
Mail Stop 1000
Fort Collins, CO 80521

Urban Ministries
1551 Regency Ct.
Calumet City, IL 60409

Warner Press, Inc.
1200 E. 5th St.
PO Box 2499
Anderson, IN 46108

Wesleyan Publishing House
8050 Castleway Dr.
PO Box 50434
Indianapolis, IN 46250

WordAction Publishing Co.
2923 Troost Ave.
Kansas City, MO 64109

Selecting Methods

*"God, after He spoke long ago to the fathers in the prophets in many portions and in many ways, in these last days has spoken to us in His Son."
(Hebrews 1:1,2)*

The prophets used some creative methods—role play, family life illustrations, storytelling, object lessons, dialectic questions, music, drama, and sermons. God used them to communicate His message. Rarely were these teachers ignored, even if their message was not popular.

Look at our teaching methods! A sign at the beginning of a long road, in the sand hills of my home state, reads, "Choose your rut carefully. You'll be in it the next 20 miles!" I recommend creative choices to my fellow church teachers with this reminder, "There is no such thing as a bad method, except the one you use all the time!"

Can we be more effective teachers by broadening our repertoire of methods? The answer is yes, if we follow sound guidelines in selecting our methods.

Principles for Selection of Methods

The objective—The most important question to ask when choosing methods is whether the approach accomplishes your aims. Students may have fun and be involved; however, if you are not accomplishing your objectives, the methods are not effective. You must choose methods that enhance your students' learning. There are many ways to add fresh insight, gain student interest, and invigorate your teaching. Variety may be more effective than the common approach to reach your aim. Do not think there is only one way to obtain your goal.

The content—Another important factor shaping method choice is the content of the lesson. Some lessons will be unfamiliar to your students. You may wish to emphasize significant information. The method is shaped by the topic, passage, or nature of the content.

Time—Limitations of time may cause students to feel stressful and rushed. Student involvement often requires more time than teacher-directed methods. To accomplish your goal, you must allot sufficient time to the technique of choice.

Available resources—Availability of resources will dictate what methods you use. A lack of art supplies, paper, pencil, or appropriate personnel will stifle a creative teaching method for various reasons. Sometimes churches do not budget adequately for supplies.

The students—The age, development, gender, and mindset of your learners influence selection of methods. You would not choose a creative writing exercise with preschool children and adults have an aversion to finger paints. Perhaps your girls are more auditory in learning or your boys display more kinesthetic skills. Most students want some innovation; however, exercise caution. Do not shock learners. Sometimes teachers feel they have to have a "bigger and better hunt" every class time. Shock may get your students attention, but these techniques rarely hold. Take care to balance your methods with the expectations of your students. Introduce your class to new methods, much like you would introduce a visitor with whom you want them to connect.

The teacher—Sometimes a teacher does not have enough skill, confidence, or knowledge to use a new method effectively. Practicing, watching other teachers, reading books on teaching, and experimenting will help expand your skills and confidence.

Purpose for Selecting Methods

Why should we try new methods? We commonly teach the way we have been taught! Even if the way we have been taught has proven effective for many students, it may not be the best for all students. Looking at current research, new teaching paradigms have emerged enabling us to better serve our students. As servant-teachers we desire the most for our students. Therefore, the most compelling reasons for new methodology are focused on the unique way God has created each student.

Matching learning styles—Research about learning styles motivates teachers to adjust their methods. Students display profound differences. Marlene LeFever, in *Learning Styles, Reaching Everyone God Gave You to Teach*, writes about four learning styles and how to teach them:

> *Imaginative Learners* ask the question "Why study this topic?" These students get involved with others and learn best in settings that allow interpersonal relationships to develop.
>
> *Analytic Learners* ask "What do I need to know about this topic?" These students learn by watching and listening. They expect a teacher to be the primary

information giver, while they carefully assess the value of the information presented.

Common Sense Learners ask "How useful to me is what I learned today?" These students like to play with ideas to see if they are rational and workable. These students want to test theory in the real world, applying what they learned.

Dynamic Learners ask "What can I do with what I've learned?" These students enjoy action, rather than analysis for their learning process. They excel in following hunches and sensing new directions and possibilities.[1]

Addressing learning domains—Students learn in three different dimensions (as described in Chapter 5: know, feel, do). To teach cognitive aims, we choose methods like lecture, simulation games, observation trips, or question and answer. When we dealing with the attitude, or affective domain, methods such as discussion, panel-forum, debate, and self-evaluation will give the footing for evaluation of various ideas. In the focus toward the behavioral domain, methods like role play, symposium, buzz groups, and brainstorming will be productive.[2]

Filling natural senses—Teaching to include something appealing to our sight, sound, touch, smell, and taste is a challenge, especially in youth and adult classes. It is, however, possible. For example, reenact a wedding to teach the book of Hosea. Most lasting and unique lessons come from employing as many senses as possible.

Fitting modality channels—Some learners achieve best through the auditory channel. Others prefer visuals to enhance their learning. Tactile-kinesthetic (or movement) learners can only master a subject after they have involved themselves in it.[3] Young children are mostly in the movement mode. As they enter school, the ability to visualize emerges as their strongest learning modality. Then, as adolescence looms, others switch their preferred style to an auditory mode.[4]

Wise teachers are aware of each learner's style and adapt lesson approaches to it. Most teachers will need to include auditory, visual, and movement methods in each lesson. Auditory methods include lecture, book reports, listening teams, and circle response. Visual methods include cartoons, coloring, reading, and field trip. Examples of kinesthetic methods are action games, collage, inductive study, and learning centers.[5] Some methods seem to cross over all modalities, e.g., storytelling, drama, and music.

Accommodating seven intelligences—Howard Gardner's seven intelligences provide fresh challenges to how people learn.[6] Akin to learning modalities, the seven intelligences are preferred ways of cognitive learning. For the more experienced teacher, adapting to the seven intelligences could be a superb way of developing greater skill in teaching.[7]

Variety in choosing methods is preferred—Fresh approaches improve our teaching. We become more innovative by evaluating our teaching style, perhaps partnering with another growing teacher. Examine past lesson plans for clues of improvement. Many teachers organize their methods into categories. Kenn Gangel's classic book *24 Ways to Improve Your Teaching* describes five such categories for teaching methods:

1. Teacher to student communication (lecture, storytelling, demonstrations).
2. Two-way communication (question and answer, discussion).
3. Group activities (panels, debates, buzz groups).
4. Instructive play (puppets, puzzles, games).
5. Non-classroom activities (field trips, guided research, projects).[8]

Other teachers find it helpful to organize methods under three divisions:

1. Teacher-centered
2. Group-centered
3. Student-centered

Teacher-Centered Methods

The first cluster of methodologies revolves around the instructor. These methods enable the teacher to direct and share information, primarily addressing the cognitive domain.

Lecture—Lectures are the organized presentation of information by the teacher via a monologue. Teachers use lecture perhaps more than any other method. It is economical in time and effort, transfers much information, and is adaptable to various sized groups. It is safe for the teacher, because he or she retains control of direction and process. Eggen and Kauchak warn lecturers about ineffectiveness with unmotivated learners.[9] This is also why Martha Leypoldt says, "Never, never, never lecture, unless there is no other way to help persons learn... The lecture is the easiest way for the teacher, but the most difficult one for the student."[10]

Enhanced lecture—Lecture continues to be the mainstay of instruction. There are ways we can make the lecture more effective. Using illustrations and visuals, you can hold students' attention. Many teachers provide an outline or note-taking handouts. Above all, keep your audience involved.

Question and answer—A better way to modify a teaching session from lecture is to use the question and answer approach. Most of the time, the teacher will prepare the questions. If you feel comfortable, students can sometimes construct thought-provoking and instructive questions. Writing questions is a skill, and any effort spent refining it is well worth the effort.

Storytelling—One of the most enjoyable teacher-centered methods is storytelling. A story, real or created, is an entertaining way to share an experience, event, or lifechange account. Jesus' use of the story was masterful. To prepare a personal experience, historical event, or biblical narrative for presentation to a class is a profoundly effective method.

Other recommended methods—Other teacher-centered methods, such as testing or evaluation, can be a learning experience. Team teaching joins the efforts of another teacher to maximize styles. Memorization and recitation, perhaps less popular, are still effective teaching approaches.

Group-Centered Methods

Group-centered methods involve less control from the teacher and use group dynamics. These methodologies better address motivational issues and the affective domain. They call for greater participation from the students.

Discussion—Dialogue about a topic may be as simple as doing a "neighbor nudge." Posing a question to discuss with others creates interaction with the content. LaFever refers to this as "a learning imperative."[11]

Simulation games—Similar to extended case studies, the entire group is involved with this approach. Sometimes called "instructive play" in the younger-aged literature, much can be gained from this guided interaction. Two helpful guidelines are (1) to secure enough staff to control the play and (2) always debrief after the formal simulation.

Buzz groups—Buzz groups take the form of releasing an entire group for creative discussion to solve a problem. The goal is to get a class "buzzing" or adding information from a variety of angles.

Listening teams—With so many fine videos and computer presentations available, a teacher must clearly outline what each team should be watching for in the presentation. Often whole group responses provide a rich arena of interaction.

Other recommended methods—Any group activity such as a panel, debate, or inclusive drama may be considered. Role playing can also be an effective group stimulus. Case studies provide insightful experience at low cost and high effect. Group projects, such as videotaping teams, observation and reporting, construction, collages, and service projects allow groups to flex their spiritual muscles.

Student-Centered Methods

Students are at the true center of all methods. More individualized than the two previous categories, student-centered methods focus creative efforts and provide more specific application. Tailored learning experiences become possible. Expertise in student-centered methods will produce maximum impact in the lives of class members if competition and community are kept in balance.

Research and reports—Although a group research project can be valuable, investigating a specific topic and returning to share with class members is an excellent independent learning experience. Often called the discovery method or an inductive study, this process works best if sound parameters are established before research begins.

Creative writing—Many forms of creative writing are helpful— paraphrase, written prayers, news articles, memos, bumper stickers, and so on. Usually more effective for older elementary, teens, and adults, this method sparks discovery and insight.

Drama, skits, and pantomimes—An exciting approach is to prepare or spontaneously produce a play, a skit, or a mime. All ages respond to the involvement and learning of dramatic presentations.

Art, craft, and music—Learning centers based on arts, crafts, or music have been effectively used with children for many years. Curriculum materials referring to "Bible Learning Centers" often utilize this method.[12] Adults are frequently surprised with enjoyment of learning through the arts. Original compositions uncover many talents.

Other recommended methods—Computer games, simulations, Internet research, interactive videos, cassettes, CDs, and other media provide a wealth of learning experiences readily available for the high-tech teacher. More modest efforts include reading assignments, projects, memory work, and interviews.

Let's Get Practical

Improving your lessons by choosing new methods is not difficult. Review the methods described in this chapter, or obtain resources listed in the bibliography. Choose at least one new method or technique to strengthen your repertoire of teaching. Ask another teacher or a class member to pray with you as you try new methods.

For Further Discussion

1. What methods did God use to teach His people in the Old Testament?
2. List the variety of methods you have used within the last three months. What observations do you conclude about your selection?

3. Review the various learning styles and modalities described in the Purpose section. From the description given, what kind of learner are you? How does this influence your teaching?
4. With which methods (listed in this chapter) are you most familiar? What one new method would you like to try? When?
5. Look ahead to next month's teaching. What new approach could you introduce to your class to enhance their learning?

Other Teaching Resources

Chuck Edwards, *Creative Teaching Techniques...for All Teachers*, video and seminar packet. Lynchburg: Sunday School Dynamics, 1994.

Wes Haystead, *Design for Teaching Teens*. Cincinnati: Standard Publishing Company, 1993. Same series has Young Children, Children, and Adults seminar videos and notebooks.

Notes

1. Marlene LeFever, *Learning Styles, Reaching Everyone God Gave You to Teach* (Colorado Springs: David C. Cook Publishing Company, 1995), 20-21, 95.
2. Marjie Mehlis, *To Teach a Teacher* (Elgin, IL: David C. Cook Publishing Company, 1978), p. 7, Transparency 7.
3. Paul Welter, *How to Help a Friend* (Wheaton: Tyndale House Publishers, 1978), 189-195.
4. LeFever, *Learning Styles*, 99-100.
5. Marcia Gillis, Patty Crowley, and Don Gillis, eds., *High Impact Teaching: Effective Lesson Planning*, video and book (Fort Worth: Resources For Ministry, 1990).
6. Howard Gardner, *Frames of Mind: The Theory of Multiple Intelligences* (New York: Basic Books, 1983), 1. Linguistic Intelligence, 2. Musical Intelligence, 3. Logical-Mathematical Intelligence, 4. Spatial Intelligence, 5. Bodily-Kinesthetic Intelligence, 6. Intrapersonal Intelligence, 7. Interpersonal Intelligence.
7. Barbara Bruce, *7 Ways to Teach the Bible to Children* (Nashville: Abingdon Press, 1996).
8. Kenneth O. Gangel, *24 Ways to Improve Your Teaching* (Wheaton: Victor Books, 1986), 9-10.
9. Paul D. Eggen and Donald P. Kauchak, *Strategies of Teachers, Teaching Content and Thinking Skills* (Boston: Allyn and Bacon, 1996), 9-10.
10. Martha M. Leypoldt, *Learning is Change, Adult Education in the Church* (Valley Forge: Judson Press, 1971, 1978), 82.
11. Marlene LeFever, *Creative Teaching Methods* (Colorado Springs: Cook Ministry Resources, 1985, 1996), 202.
12. Barbara J. Boulton et al, *How to Do Bible Learning Activities*, Early Childhood I & II, Children I & II, Youth, and Adults (Ventura: Gospel Light Publications, 1982).

Preparing Materials

"Be diligent to present yourself approved to God as a workman who does not need to be ashamed, handling accurately the word of truth." (2 Timothy 2:15)

If you ever build a house, you will discover it takes as much time to secure construction documents and build the foundation as it does to erect the house. Teaching has many similarities. The development cycle for a curriculum is typically three years. A teacher's preparation is often a week's work, followed by the actual teaching time. Depending on the specific church program, your students receives 25 to 50 minutes of classtime to reap the benefits of diligent men and women involved with the process.

This chapter explores the teacher's task to prepare materials for instruction. In addition to gaining perspective and setting appropriate preparation priorities, teachers need to establish inexpensive supplies. Churches should provide most items to teachers.

Perspective, Priorities, and Preparation Time

Three ingredients are essential to be a successful teacher. First, a teacher must understand God's *perspective* on the ministry of teaching. Those who serve in Christian education do so as ambassadors for Christ. At times, we forget the importance of our role as teachers. Teaching is the foundation on which an entire generation builds its view of God and His grace for the world! Teaching is not something we accept because no one else volunteers. Our calling to teach is part of God's desire and plan to change the world.

God's perspective helps us establish our *priorities*. When a teacher realizes the tremendous responsibility of shepherding a class, adjustments to priorities in life will occur. The successful teacher realizes the time commitment to teaching may involve saying no to other opportunities. No one can expect to do everything. Teaching to change lives is one of the most important ways to invest yourself. It requires time and energy.

An important job, logically, suggests *preparation time.* After all, Bible teaching carries eternal consequences. Good preparation cannot be achieved within 10 minutes before class. Good preparation involves a lifestyle of healthy priorities! So, what does good preparation imply?

A prepared teacher knows the students well—An hour once a week (although filled with worship, learning activities, and the Bible lesson) leaves little time to get acquainted with students. A teacher who especially wants to impact someone's life must first know the challenges each person will face. A great blessing for a teacher is the opportunity to contact students outside class time:

—During a church potluck.

—A telephone call to ask how school is going.

—Attending a musical or sports event involving the student.

—Sending a birthday card.

—Visiting the family in their home.

—Hosting pizza parties.

Gain a better understanding of your class any way possible. A successful teacher takes the time and makes opportunities to demonstrate care for students.

A prepared teacher prays for students—A practical tool for organizing your prayer ministry is a stack of lined note cards. Place a different student's name, family information, address, phone number, and prayer requests on each card. Divide the cards into seven piles and secure with a rubber band. You now have a bundle for each day to direct your prayer time for the week. Some teachers pray for their students while commuting to and from work. Others systematically pray as part of their devotional time. This may not seem like classroom preparation, but it is the most important aspect any successful teacher undertakes.

A prepared teacher is a student of the Word—Relationships are one dimension of preparation. Handling the Word is another. A successful teacher systematically studies God's Word for personal growth and maturity as well to teach the lesson to others. Practically speaking, as a teacher establishes priorities for life, the need to set aside regular study time must be a critical item. The length of time and the time of day will vary with each teacher. It is important to read, meditate, and seek God's favor for every portion of the lesson. The teacher's guide, from printed curriculum materials, will provide valuable insight into the selected Bible passage. Teachers use a good Bible commentary, Bible atlas, Bible dictionary, and several different Bible translations in preparing content. It is also wise for the teacher to memorize the key verse if students will be asked to memorize. Example provides positive motivation for students!

A prepared teacher organizes lesson materials—There are enough distractions in a classroom without disorganization on the part of the teacher. A thorough teacher thinks through all the resources needed during the class hour. Many publishers provide a list of resources needed for each lesson. Experienced teachers know, however, that the publisher cannot anticipate everything regarding your classroom. So, make your own list and check it twice! Determine which items are presently in your classroom and which items are not. Take responsibility for collecting or verifying that all the items you need are in your classroom. Discipline yourself to not forget anything when you leave home.

Depending on the age of your students, part of a teacher's preparation may be handout papers. Tearing worksheets from student books (for children) or photocoping outlines (for older students) helps your audience stay focused on the specific lesson for the week. Maximize teaching time with functions such as pre-assembly of craft project items or scheduling individuals to provide and serve snacks. Parents are prime candidates to assist in children's areas.

Finally, *a prepared teacher makes the classroom setting ready for students*—This implies that the teacher thinks about and adjusts classroom furniture, the temperature, the light, the bulletin boards, and any other item that will impact sensory perception. In working with children, it is wise to create posters to place in the room that identify the schedule of a "normal" class experience. These posters designate activities and time references. They provide structure for the hour and guide workers as well as children throughout the hour. Be specific with scheduling (especially if you post the class hour) to include expected time for singing, snacks, crafts, teaching and learning activities, bathroom breaks, share and prayer time, etc. Most importantly, good preparation means leaving home early to be in the classroom with everything arranged before students arrive.

Inexpensive Supplies to Inventory

Classroom supplies are always a challenge. Many churches assign one individual to function like a purchasing agent. In this case, one person buys all regular supplies (in bulk) and maintains a standardized inventory of weekly supplies for each classroom. Other churches expect teachers to maintain their own supplies. It is important to clarify with Christian education leadership the church's policies and expectations. Teachers should also clarify what budget restraints and procedures are in place. It is not wise for a church to expect teachers to purchase their own supplies from personal funds. Teaching budgets must be designed to stock supportive tools and supplies as well as curriculum materials.

Consider necessary items in two categories. The first category includes general supplies in each classroom. A second category involves specialized or age-appropriate supplies that may be stored in a central supply room. Often, churches create an instructional resource room in conjunction with the church library to track equipment and specialty items shared over the teaching year. Resources and equipment in this second category are usually more expensive and need a higher level of security within the church facility.

Although different locations will create different lists, below are sample categories of typical Christian education supplies. The challenge is not creating the list; the challenge is maintaining the inventories so that no teacher arrives for class to find her classroom supplies cupboard raided or empty.

General Supplies for Each Classroom
  Children
  Brass paper fasteners (sometimes called "brads")
  Construction paper (variety of colors) and drawing paper (white)
  Lined writing paper
  Cotton balls
  White glue
  Rubber cement
  Clear adhesive tape
  Colored markers (water soluble–8 colors are sufficient)
  Crayons (8 colors are sufficient)
  Sharpened pencils
  Safety scissors for students
  Scissors for teacher/helpers
  Basic first aid kit
  Cleaning supplies

  Teens and Adults
  Music
  Extra Bibles
  Paper
  Pencils

Specialized and Age-Appropriate Supplies
  Books (age-appropriate)
  Audio cassette tape player(s)
  Liquid tempera paint (8 colors), with bowls and brushes
      for classroom tables
  Toys (appropriate for nursery and preschool)
  Drinking straws (for crafts)
  Wooden craft sticks (for crafts)
  Role (mural) paper–several different colors (for bulletin
      boards)

Bulletin board borders (thematic for the year)
Church graphics/clip art books
Large current world maps and Bible times maps
Teaching puppets
Flannel graph Bible story set (Betty Lukens type)
Flannel graph boards with easels
Videotape player/television unit on rolling cart
Videotape library (Bible stories and life application stories)
Overhead projector(s) on rolling cart(s)
Photocopier and supplies for transparencies
Instant camera and extra film
Parachute (for fun!)

Let's Get Practical

Organization implies competence to others. Teaching preparation time must include regular attention to the details of an efficient classroom experience. Determine fully the expectations of your ministry and subdivide the workload throughout the week. Solicit help from others if necessary. Initially the system you design requires time for refinement. Each teacher must develop his or her own schedule for classroom preparation. Once in place, weekly duties are performed with confidence and honor to your calling.

For Further Discussion

1. How do you organize a systematic prayer program for your students?
2. How long do you spend in study for your lesson? Can you present it without using your teacher's guide? How long do you think a successful teacher prepares for class?
3. List the supplies in your classroom and compare your list to the classroom supply list in this chapter. What items would you add?
4. What is your budget for supplies? If you do not know, who can you ask to find out?
5. Develop a personal schedule for teaching responsibilities. What activities would you eliminate from your life-style so you can adequately prepare for teaching?

Setting Your Classroom

"By wisdom a house is built, and by understanding it is established; And by knowledge the rooms are filled with all precious and pleasant riches." (Proverbs 24:3,4)

One definition of environment is "the totality of surrounding conditions and circumstances affecting growth and development."[1] Examine the following scenarios:

> An Ukrainian student struggles for grades in a Nebraska classroom. He has difficulty with comprehension until the teacher observes his squinting. A trip to the eye doctor soon follows, and behold, Sasha is back on track.

> A group of adults crowds into a Sunday school class as a result of good instruction and leadership from the teacher. Each week the room is warm, stuffy, and cramped. As the situation persists, attendance begins to dwindle. Moving to another room, with better ventilation and more floor space, allows the class to thrive and grow again.

> A club leader determines over one-third of her 4th and 5th graders have experienced divorce in the last several years. Also, most of the families have moms who work outside the home. She sets aside time to talk with each student about their stresses and pray together. Soon the entire club functions better.

Physical environment prompts consideration of seating arrangements, lighting, and decor. Instructional environment concerns the placement of media and students for maximum learning effectiveness. Psychological environment influences teaching even when it is difficult to control. Therefore, adjust your teaching to current happenings in the lives of students.

Physical Environment–Facility

Facility—To illustrate this dilemma, imagine a country church, whose members averaged 60 years of age. It was awkwardly constructed. Fourteen steep steps climbed to the sanctuary. Visitors were always confused with the maze-like instructions for locating the gym. The enthusiastic, and youthful, building committee could not understand why the architect resisted the idea of a basement until he explained how difficult it was for senior citizens.

Issues such as visibility, parking, disabled access (30 million disabled people in the United States alone[2]), have much to do with the learning activity. Sometimes we cannot do anything about the location. At other times, something as simple as posting signs to direct people to classrooms can make a difference. Prepare people for greeting and ushering duties. When the time comes for more drastic measures, remodeling may be necessary to facilitate the designated activity.

Space—How much room should you plan for students? Space should be large enough to accommodate your class comfortably. A general rule is:

30 square feet per child (early childhood and elementary),
20 square feet for youth,
15 square feet for adults.

Rooms with 800-900 square feet are suggested because they hold the average number of students. Wes Haystead explains that standard-sized rooms service all age groups because older students do not require as much space, yet, the maximum grouping size increases.[3]

Visual conditions—Have you ever been seated behind a tall person when the teacher was very short? Have you ever struggled to read a book at sunset as the sky gradually grew darker? If so, you understand the importance of proper visual angles and lighting. Students need enough light to see, without obstructions, at a proper distance from visual aids. Wall color can be of assistance. Usually lighter colors encourage participation and attention. Darker colors provide more somber settings. Another cause for conflict is the decoration in classrooms. Some argue that pictures and posters in a classroom will distract students or mar the walls.

Auditory conditions—A room filled with distractions, noise, interruptions, and projection problems will hinder learning for any age. When teaching older adults, assisted hearing devices are a kind gesture. Echoes off unfinished walls, microphone feedback, or lack of amplification frustrate students (and most teachers)!

Age Group	Maximum Attendance Per Department	Optimum Room Dimensions	Floor Space Per Person	Teacher/Learner Ratio, Small Group
Early Childhood Ages 0-1	12-15	24' x 36' = 900 sq. ft.	30-35 sq. ft.	1:4
Ages 2-3	16-20	24' x 36' = 900 sq. ft.	30-35 sq. ft.	1:5
Ages 4-5	20-24	24' x 36' = 900 sq. ft.	30-35 sq. ft.	1:6
Children Grades 1-6	25-30	24' x 36' = 900 sq. ft.	25-30 sq. ft.	1:6-8
Youth Grades 7-12	30-40	24' x 36' = 900 sq. ft.	20-25 sq. ft.	1:8
Adults	30-40	18' x 25' = 450 sq. ft.	10-15 sq. ft.	1:6 (Care groups)

These specific guidelines for space allocation are from Lowell Brown[4]

Personal comfort conditions—Reduce fatigue and nurture attention by the furnishings you select. Purchase comfortable chairs, tables and/or desks that encourage interaction. Instructional media devices increase concentration. Bulletin boards and displays are helpful. They should be at your learners' eye level. Lighting, air, and temperature are equally essential concerns. Many excellent lessons are ruined by drowsy minds or shivering bodies. Room temperature is important!

Maintenance and evaluation—Failure to regularly inspect and repair facilities and furnishings will hinder learning. It conveys an image of incompetence. Neglect is poor stewardship when easily repaired items are unusable.

Preparation—Learning is already diminished when students enter a dark and unsupervised room. "Previous planning prevents poor performance" is a sound guideline for the environment we need to create. You may not have elaborate provisions but you can be prepared to use whatever is available to accomplish excellent learning goals. Good teachers are in charge of their classrooms.

Instructional Environment–Furnishings

How should you utilize the furnishings of a classroom? Surprisingly, the "set up" says much about the stewardship, philosophy of learning, image, and expected activity of the class. Equipment serves as tools for the ministry. Furniture can either enhance or inhibit teaching.

Arrangement—Few classrooms have fixed seating anymore. Flexibility to move (so all students can see, hear, and participate) helps the teacher considerably. Try arranging desks or chairs in a deep "V" or a semicircle. More daring teachers will experiment with "teaching in the round." When room arrangements are flexible, you will feel free to incorporate creative Bible learning methods.

Image viewing—Few things are more frustrating than trying to see a screen, whiteboard, video, or computer-generated presentation with people or objects in the way. Dimming the lights for a filmstrip or computer projector may guarantee inattention. Films, overhead projectors, and other presentations at the front of the room should be bright and high enough to be seen by all. Screens are viewed best within a minimum distance of twice the width and a maximum distance of 10 times the width. Also, front projection screens are usually best when viewed from a 45-degree angle—no more.

Grouping factors—As the size of your group increases, poor discipline and low student participation can lead the list of problems. On the other hand, in youth and adult settings large groups can generate energy, provide diversity, and give a feeling of anonymous security. An appropriately sized group will achieve better instruction than too large a group. Crowded classrooms are exciting for a brief time, but lose effectiveness rapidly.

Student participation— Student involvement has already been cited with the placement of furniture. Another factor is psychological, as discusssed in the next section. Many of us remember negative childhood experiences as we developed through various stages when age, gender, or other similarities or differences seriously effected learning.

Equipment—By looking at our abundant accessibility to multimedia today, we can conclude there are many options. Use media to increase efficiency and effectiveness.

Psychosocial Environment–Feelings

Interestingly, "one in four church attenders say new Christians may not feel comfortable in their Sunday school." How do we address this discomfort? Some say we are not members of God's family to be comfortable. However the spirit of grace and caring toward others, whether inside or outside of faith, is Christlike conduct. Even though we cannot make people's problems disappear, we can give them hope that the Lord will change their lives. Understanding the psychosocial environment is important to the learning and growth of students. What are some factors?

Home and family influences—Family situations, and the responsibilities they create, influence learning in the classroom. Homelife issues often force us to adapt our teaching and deal with some issues directly. At other times, we are simply aware of needs and available for prayer and support.

Work and school influences—Time requirements of work or school, and its accompanying stress, present unique challenges. Issues like sudden unemployment, job/school transfer, return to the work force, or demands of extracurricular school events, all effect intellectual and spiritual growth. Although such things are commonly negative, it is possible for education to occur *because of* these influences.

Community influences—Some communities have a high regard for Christian education while others ridicule it. The economic strength, the quality of social services, and community norms can either facilitate a positive learning environment or detract from it.

Cultural influences—A person's political, racial, and educational background must be reconciled with Scripture. The Bible warns against separating Christians with unwarranted barriers of race, economics, etc. (James 2:1-4; Gal. 3:28; Col. 3:11).

Spiritual influences—The Bible describes a spiritual battlefield (Eph. 6:12) where Christians confront the forces of darkness. Spiritual battles are won with prayer. Teachers and students must pray for each other.

Nature of classrooms—Classroom environments are multidimensional. A variety of unpredictable things do not necessarily detract from the learning experience. Although teachers intuitively know these characteristics exist, often we forget how these affect our teaching. The teacher must be prepared to quickly adapt to changing conditions during the class session.

Let's Get Practical

The teacher must be aware of both the internal and external environments of the teaching process. While the internal environment is easier to control, often resources are not available to achieve the ideal classroom. The effective teacher will seek creative ways to deal with less than ideal physical conditions.

The internal, psychosocial environment is more difficult to manage. However, the teacher must attempt to keep current with all internal influences on teacher and student alike. The primary resource available to the Christian teacher is the insight and empowerment of the Holy Spirit. The teacher fully yielded to the Holy Spirit will be able to adapt to constantly changing classroom conditions.

For Further Discussion

1. In what physical environments did Jesus teach? What psychosocial environments? What insights do you gain from these observations?
2. What hindrances to growth and development can you observe in your instructional setting? What can you do about it?
3. If you were to do a facility audit, what areas would be most commendable? Which would be least commendable?
4. What grouping and student participation expectations do your teachers have? Are they shaping their environment or being shaped by it?
5. What is the profile of a typical student in your class? What home, work, community, and cultural influences are effecting instruction?

Notes

1. *Electronic Thesaurus*, based upon *The American Heritage Dictionary* (New York: Houghton Mifflin Co., 1995).
2. Jim Pierson and Robert E. Korth, eds., *Special People, A Resource from Ministry with Persons Who Have Disabilities* (Cincinnati: Standard Publishing, 1989), 141.
3. Haystead, *The 21st Century Sunday School.*
4. Brown, *Sunday School Standards.*
5. *The 1997 David C. Cook National Survey On the Impact of Sunday School* (Colorado Springs: David C. Cook Church Ministries, 1997), Fact 9.

Evaluating Teaching

"Test yourselves to see if you are in the faith; examine yourselves! Or do you not recognize this about yourselves, that Jesus Christ is in you—unless indeed you fail the test." (2 Corinthians 13:5)

Evaluation is important in Christian education for both students and teachers. Evaluation is the process of comparing a present condition with a desired condition for the purpose of continuing, changing, or creating new directions. It focuses attention on whether or not we have met our goals. Teachers need to know if their students are progressing toward the goal of spiritual maturity. Teachers also need to know if they are living up to their own potential as teachers.

Often, evaluation is viewed as a negative experience. Some view it as dealing only with what is wrong in a student or teacher. While evaluation can be misused in this way, the main purpose of the process is to provide positive feedback and should ultimately result in encouraging the student or teacher.

Most importantly, evaluation is important for the Christian because of the many passages which teach we are being evaluated by God now and will be evaluated by Him in the life to come (Rom. 14:9-12; 1 Cor. 3:11-15; 11:27-31; 2 Tim. 4:6-8).

Elements of Evaluation

Whether for students or teachers, evaluation consists of three basic elements:

Present condition—Evaluation is concerned with the truth about a student or a teacher. While we should have a sensitivity to "speaking the truth in love" (Eph. 4:15), to be helpful evaluation must be based on reality.

Desired condition—Evaluation must be based on comparing what is with what should or ought to be. In other words, evaluation begins with the goals we have for our students and ourselves as teachers. Each Bible teaching program in the church should have general and specific goals for each age group. Lowell Brown reminds us this is a two-step process:

1. Identifying why your teaching program exists;
2. Determining standards that measure the effectiveness of your program in fulfilling its purpose.[1]

For the teacher, the evaluation process begins when the teacher receives a *ministry description* at the beginning of the term of service. The ministry description sets forth what is expected of the teacher, the basic criteria by which the teacher will be evaluated, and when and how the evaluation will take place. Thus, from day one, the teacher knows exactly what is expected and that an evaluation will take place.

New directions—New directions refer to the desired result of the evaluation process. Properly done, evaluation will assist in charting the future of our teaching. These new directions may include new patterns of teaching, new methods of relating to students, modifications in teaching procedures, as well as ideas on how teaching can be improved.

Often the tendency is to continue what we have been doing, especially if we feel it is effective or has not yet reached its full impact. At other times, we are anxious to change what we are doing; to find better ways of accomplishing our goals and try them. Evaluation may discover it is time to discontinue a program or method. When we observe a pattern has accomplished its purpose, hinders other goals, or is simply not connected to any purpose, then it is time to stop. Sometimes evaluation reveals we are not doing something that we could or should be doing. It is at this time we should create new patterns, procedures, or programs.

Purposes of Evaluation

We assess our teaching to gain confidence, skill, and enthusiasm. Evaluation tells us what we are doing right and what we need to improve. The examination exercise reveals several purposes of accomplishment.

Student growth—"We proclaim Him, admonishing and teaching everyone with all wisdom, so that we may present everyone perfect in Christ" (Col. 1:28). If we examine what is going on in our students' lives, we can promote their growth and development.

Program effectiveness—Have resources been used wisely? Do we need more resources? Do we have productive interaction between students and teacher? These questions pertain to the class' effectiveness. "The basic purpose of educational evaluation is to determine the effectiveness of the educational program to improve the quality of teaching and learning."[2] Evaluation can determine needed changes, creations, or continuations.

Teacher development—Observing teachers in action helps them improve their practices and techniques. Wilhoit and Ryken outline the tasks of an effective teacher as:

> Fostering active learning, motivating students, clarifying communication, challenging students, making class minutes count, focusing on the big idea, making the truth personal, building a constructive class atmosphere, and distinguishing between major and minor issues.[3]

Evaluation helps the beginning teacher gain confidence and the more experienced teacher to continue improving. Evaluation also helps pacing, even for a master teacher. To mentor and train other teachers is obedience to God's intent for ministry.

Doctrinal accuracy—This may seem like an intrusive purpose of evaluation, but it has been a practice since biblical times. In relation to the ministry of Apollos, "This man had been instructed in the way of the Lord, and being fervent in spirit, he was speaking and teaching accurately the things concerning Jesus...But when Priscilla and Aquila heard him, they took him aside and explained to him the way of God more accurately" (Acts 18:25,26). Evaluation is the first step in this process.

Administrative information—Evaluation helps those in charge of supervision to function more effectively and make informed decisions. Evaluation impacts the planning process. The goals of the ministry leader in evaluation include making sure the teacher is operating within the sphere of personal giftedness, there is a good "fit" between the teacher and students, determining if further training and equipping is needed and how to provide it, as well as providing the resources needed to improve the quality of the teaching.

Types of Evaluation

Formative evaluation—When we discuss what curriculum to use next quarter or how to make our students feel at ease in Bible study, we are doing formative evaluation. We are getting ready to teach. This type of evaluation takes place before the actual teaching time. Do not rush this kind of evaluation. Allow it to produce the purposes listed above.

Concurrent evaluation—This kind of evaluation happens during the class session every time we teach. Teachers should constantly look for indications that students are grasping the truths presented. If they are not, concurrent evaluation prompts the teacher to make the needed adjustments. When we evaluate ourselves while we are teaching, we do not need to wait for another day to improve. We can adapt our teaching to the current conditions.

Summative evaluation—This type of evaluation is used to assess what has happened in the teaching session and thus looks backward. While each teacher should spend some time in summative evaluation after each teaching experience, this is also the type of evaluation that takes place at least annually in conjunction with the ministry leadership. In a sense, summative evaluation will move into formative evaluation as the cycle of these three types of evaluation continues with the teaching process.

Sources of Evaluation

Observation—Where does one get the information to make evaluation about teaching and learning? Observation is the most common route. A Sunday school superintendent, for example, can visit classrooms with a checklist of important items, or just to see what happens in the session without preset specifications. Sometimes it is valuable to invite an experience teacher, from outside your church, to come in for consultation. Some Bible colleges and seminaries will provide evaluation teams, made up of faculty and/or students, who come to a church to observe and evaluate the educational processes.

Testing—Amazingly, we expect our public and Christian schools (and home schooling) to measure progress by testing and grading the individual student. Yet, when it comes to Christian education in the church, we say it is impossible to measure what happens spiritually. When it is difficult to observe comprehension, it may be helpful to use testing as an evaluation tool. Give care to test accurately. Some students will profit from the review for an exam.

Visits and family interaction—Too often teachers neglect the value of a home visit. "The best insights are frequently obtained through a brief, personal visit to a person's home or place of employment."[4] One youth pastor told his teaching team if they only had three hours a week to invest in preparation, to do so as follows: one hour in prayer, one hour in study, and one hour in contacting youth "on their turf." This is good advice for teachers of any age group.

Research—Formal study of student growth under controlled conditions is slowly becoming a part of some Christian education. If we have the resources, we may do this ourselves. However, sometimes publishing companies will prepare and distribute reports regarding the issues of teaching in Christian education. Keeping up with a few of the major publishers may be well worth your time as a teacher.

Written inventories and surveys—When students complete open ended and comparative questions about a class or study, surprising feedback results. We may be pleased with what the student learns and how much he or she really appreciates it. More likely, we will learn of a few areas where students affirm our efforts and a few where they feel we could improve. Many church attenders agree that their teachers need more training to be effective.[5]

Interviews—As a teacher of adults, try to interview students about their impression of class function and ways to improve application for their lives. Interviews can follow a formal structure or be more relaxed. Either is effective to gain a snapshot of learning.

Guidelines for Evaluation

Keep it simple—When you do evaluation, you should keep it as simple as possible. Many go to elaborate plans when reviewing their teaching. A complicated, multi-step process may not yield desired results but may lead to more confusion. Richard Patterson suggests evaluation be "as small as possible, as representative as necessary, and as authoritative as needed."[6]

Clarify your goals—Unstated or unclear goals of instruction will make evaluation difficult or impossible. Church leadership must be involved in setting overall goals for the Christian education program. Ministry leaders should set learning goals for each individual program and age group involved in Bible teaching. As stated earlier, this information should be included in the ministry description provided for each teacher.

Use the results—Some people resist evaluation because nothing ever seems to come of it. Make sure, when the study or teaching review is done, that it results in action. Act on what you discover as a student, teacher, or ministry leader. Teachers need encouragement to gain further confidence and improve in their skills. A usable evaluation is "inexpensive, brief, easy to administer and score, and does not interfere with other activities."[7]

Don't reinvent the wheel—Resources are abundant to help teachers improve their teaching. Some are listed at the end of this chapter. A wise teacher will use or customize resources before investing time to developing their own. This is good stewardship of time. A teacher evaluation form should cover areas such as personal preparation, motivation of students, design and direction of the teaching-learning process, personal concern for students, and participation as a team member.

Make them valid—Evaluation should look at the long-term progress of a student or teacher and not just be a one-shot exercise. If evaluation only happens once a year, you may catch a student or a teacher on a "bad day." Be sure to consider all extenuating circumstances before making major changes based on one evaluation. Keeping careful records of evaluations that happen over a period of time is the best indicator of student or teacher performance.

Let's Get Practical

Four steps follow to engage the evaluation process:

1. Establish purpose and standards for the evaluation.
2. Select the best way to get the true picture of present conditions.
3. Analyze the information and clarify who makes the decisions.
4. Communicate the results of the evaluation to interested parties.

For Further Discussion

1. Are teachers in your church or organization more likely to panic about evaluation, avoid evaluation, or achieve a balance? How can you eliminate apprehension?
2. Are purposes and standards for your Bible study or class clearly stated? How would you revise them?
3. What type of evaluation does your church or organization need for its educational endeavors?
4. What is the best way to conduct evaluation in your church or organization? Why?
5. Which guideline will be the most difficult to follow? How can you accomplish a sound evaluation?

For Further Reading

How Effective Is Your Church's Educational Ministry? Brochure published by Evangelical Training Association, 110 Bridge Street, Box 327, Wheaton, IL 60189-0327, Phone: 800-369-8291.

John R. Cionca, *Solving Church Education's Ten Toughest Problems.* Wheaton: Victor Books, 1990.

Harold J. Westing, *Evaluate & Grow.* Wheaton: Victor Books, 1984.

Notes

1. Brown, *Sunday School Standards*, 5.
2. Eldridge, *The Teaching Ministry of the Church*, 310.
3. Wilhoit and Ryken, *Effective Bible Teaching*, Chapter 2.
4. Wilkinson, *The 7 Laws of the Learner*, 260.
5. *The 1997 David C. Cook National Survey On the Impact of Sunday School*, Fact 6.
6. Richard Patterson, *Evaluating Church Education*, audio tapes (Wheaton: Evangelical Training Association, 1990).
7. James S. Cangelosi, *Evaluating Classroom Instruction* (New York: Longman, 1991), 31.

Keeping Fresh

"For Ezra had set his heart to study the law of the Lord, and to practice it, and to teach His statutes and ordinances in Israel." (Ezra 7:10)

What gives some teachers the ability to teach effectively week after week, year after year? Do these teachers ever get discouraged? If so, how do they keep going and "fulfill their ministry?" (2 Tim. 4:5). Excellent questions. Most teachers are discouraged by time pressures, inattentive students, and their own failures. But there are several qualities that, if possessed, will enable teachers to progress in their teaching ministries for a lifetime. This chapter focuses on those qualities.

The qualities we will discuss are important for both novice and experienced teachers. If practiced, these qualities will allow beginning teachers to avoid potential pitfalls. For more experienced teachers who feel they have reached a plateau and the joy of teaching is gone, these qualities can provide spiritual renewal. Teachers who have "burned-out" can develop strategies to prevent it from happening again. These qualities can help Bible teachers to stay balanced so they continue to learn today in order to continue to teach tomorrow.

A Refreshed Picture of God

Relationship—It is assumed that a Bible study leader or Sunday school teacher has a personal relationship with God through Jesus Christ. However, do not pass over this point too quickly. The Pharisees of Jesus' day were the most scripturally literate people around and they did not have a relationship with the Father (John 5:37-40). Even when we know the Lord as our personal Savior, it is still possible to need to "draw near to God, and He will draw near to you" (James 4:8). Dawson Trotman describes three reasons Christians are not reproducing spiritually: they are immature, they are allowing sin to be in their life, or they do not have union with the Savior.[1] A strong relationship with Christ is perhaps the most important quality that will keep a teacher effective. Paul's

85

warning to Timothy about false teachers highlights this point: "For some men, straying from these things, have turned aside to fruitless discussion, wanting to be teachers of the Law, although they do not understand either what they are saying or the matters about which they make confident assertions" (1 Tim. 1:6,7).

Priority—The greatest commandment is to "love the Lord your God with all your heart, and with all your soul, and with all your mind, and with all your strength" (Mark 12:30). Unfortunately, teachers can be tempted to make this verse say that we should "love the lesson of the Lord our God with all our heart..." We must develop proper focus. Nothing is more important than being in touch with God as we teach, before we teach, and after we teach. Ray and Anne Ortlund remind us "We must be the people of God before we do the work of God."[2] A stay-fresh teacher focuses on his or her relationship with God, and makes it a priority.

Dealing with sin—Nothing will curtail a teacher's effectiveness more than sin in the life of that teacher. "But your iniquities have made a separation between you and your God, and your sins have hidden His face from you, so that He does not hear" (Isa. 59:2). It will not be too long before your class or study group will know that the power is gone. Fresh effective teaching comes from a clean vessel. Guard your attitudes, because they can deter you and your class. Keep short accounts with God and others. Confess known sin quickly if you are to remain a fresh teacher (Prov. 28:13).

Spiritual disciplines—Solitude, study, meditation, prayer, fasting, worship, simplicity, confession, and stewardship are all powerful refreshers for the burned-out teacher. There are a number of excellent books which can help you learn and develop spiritual disciplines (listed at the end of this chapter). A "dry" teacher should take advantage of the rich restoring qualities of applied spiritual disciplines.

Prayer—Teachers must be people of prayer. Terrell Peace has written, "In emphasizing the technical aspects of Bible study and lesson preparation, we in no way want to lessen the part spiritual preparation plays in effective teaching."[3] Bible students should pray with their teachers. They should pray for their teachers. Teachers should pray for themselves and for their students. Occasional extended times of prayer during the class session are very beneficial. They can help you catch up with your people and for your people. Prayer will keep a teacher fresh.

Mentoring—An effective way to stay fresh is to invest in the mentoring process. "Mentoring is a relational experience in which one person empowers another by sharing God-given resources."[4] This may involve you being mentored, or you may be mentoring peers and students. Sharing your spriritual journey with others and learning from theirs is refreshing for the teacher.

A Renewed Perspective From God

Margin—Richard Swenson has defined the concept of margin as "the amount allowed beyond that which is needed...it is the leeway we once had between ourselves and our limits."[5] Margin can be physical, chronological, financial, or emotional. Too often a teacher or Christian leader commits few resources to developing a margin. Perhaps the sabbath principle described in the Old Testament was established for this very purpose: One day set aside after six for worship and rest. Is there an overload in your teaching? Once I had to admit I was teaching too many Bible studies and not enjoying them. In this case, less equaled more enjoyment!

Rest and food—When Elijah grew exhausted from ministry and depressed to the point of death, God prepared his recovery with first giving him rest and nourishment (1 Kings 19:4-8). When the disciples had been on an extensive teaching and preaching trip, Jesus took them to a solitary place to refresh and review (Mark 6:30,31). Insuring that we have proper rest and diet will eliminate a hindrance which can keep teachers from success.

Fellowship—We have been placed into the body of Christ for mutual upbuilding (Eph. 4:16). Encouragers come in a variety of shapes and sizes, but who can underestimate the power of a person speaking hope to you? Calvin Miller states "behind every dynamic man is the supporting confidence and help of his family. In a similar way, behind every great leader there is always a loyal network of a great many friends."[6] Jesus sent His disciples out by twos to minister. Elijah was told there were still faithful people who had not bowed to evil. Paul had Barnabas, David had his "mighty men," Moses his Joshua, Aaron, and Hur. Even Jesus had a close circle of three. Fellowship gives fresh perspective for the ministry work.

Avoid demotivators—Too many things can discourage a teacher from doing an effective job. Frustration with life and feeling overwhelmed can happen to the busy teacher. "Elephant stakes" are mental references that keep us from doing a good job of teaching and are sometimes hard to uproot. Fatigue can make you an ineffective teacher. Past failures will hinder your ministry if not put in proper perspective. Stifling opinions, losing focus, and stagnation are real dangers to the teacher who wants to finish well. 1 Corinthians 15:58 speaks to these negative influences, " Therefore my beloved brethren, be steadfast, immovable, always abounding in the work of the Lord, knowing that your toil is not in vain in the Lord." Effective teachers are aware of demotivators and make adjustments to overcome them.

Handling stress—All of us are faced with stress every day. It is not a question of *will* we face it but *how* will we handle it? Some amount of stress seems to help teachers do their best. However, too quickly pressures can inundate our lives. These pressures sometimes come as time constraints, financial need, relationship conflicts, and even dealing with the rigorous pace of modern life. The teacher must learn to "casting all your anxiety upon Him, because He cares for you" (1 Pet. 5:7).

A Restored Passion for Teaching

Developing others as teachers—There are few things more worthwhile than "working yourself out of a job." According to Ephesians 4:12, the role of teacher is to "equip the saints for the work of the ministry." Notice it does not say "whipping the saints!" We should not be driving our people, but developing them. Seek to have several novice teachers in each class or Bible study. Your goal should be to take them through the stages of developing leadership confidence so that they will be competent and confident teachers.

Consider a short sabbatical—When writing this book, I took a few months off from teaching a class of adults. When I came back, the class noticed a renewed vigor and freshness in my teaching. If you have been teaching for many years without a break, you should consider a few months off to recharge your batteries. And if you have been developing other teachers, you will have someone well trained to take your place!

Team teaching—One way to broaden the influence of teaching is to develop a team approach. Working with another person requires attention to communication, planning, and support and can result in a freshness to your ministry.

Reading—Reading is a rewarding way to expand your mind and ministry. As a teacher, I suggest that you read much in your field. One or more of the books listed in the end notes of this book would be a excellent place to start. Do not let the teaching fires diminish. But do not limit your reading to material directly related to your teaching. You will be amazed at how stretching and freshening reading outside your "comfort zone" can be. Consider biographies of great men and women as a way to gain new insights into life and learning.

New methods—Amazingly, a new method will increase your faith in what God will do. It will alert your students to a desire to grow. It will freshen your perspective of how to teach from new angles. Review Chapter 8 of this book and make a commitment to try at least one new method the next time you teach.

Learning—The summary of staying fresh in your teaching is to continue to grow! Howard Hendricks, who continues to teach long after others his age are on the sidelines, has written, "The effective teacher always teaches from the overflow of a full life...If you stop growing today, you stop teaching tomorrow."[7] Too many teachers retire their curiosity before they retire from teaching! The fresh teacher is not a stagnant pond, nor a dry brook. The teacher who has staying power is a continual learner.

Let's Get Practical

If you are feeling a bit "burned out" right now, pick one area above and begin to immediately implement it. Fresh teaching comes from obedient application.

For Further Discussion

1. Evaluate where you are right now in your teaching ministry. How fresh do you think you are? How fresh would your people say you are?
2. Many Scriptures are listed in this chapter. Why not take some time alone with the Lord and His Word? Look up the Scriptures and allow the Holy Spirit to illumine you.
3. How do you get a fresh picture of God when you are discouraged? Can you think of anyone in your class or study group who needs a fresh glimpse?
4. You are to be commended for making it to the end of this book! What other books could you read and further improve in this area?
5. What could you share from this book with one other teacher of the Bible? Why not set up a time to share that with the other person?

Additional Resources

Foster, Richard J. *Celebration of Discipline*. New York: Harper & Row, Publishers, 1978.

Swindoll, Charles R. *Intimacy with the Almighty*. Dallas: Word Publishing, 1996.

Whitney, Donald S. *Spiritual Disciplines for the Christian Life*. Colorado Springs: NavPress, 1991.

Willard, Dallas. *The Spirit of the Disciplines*. San Francisco: Harper & Row, Publishers, 1988.

Notes

1. Dawson Trotman, *Born to Reproduce* (Lincoln, NE: Back to the Bible Broadcast, 1975), 27.
2. Ortlund, *Renewal*, 9.
3. Terrell Peace in *The Teaching Ministry of the Church*, ed. by Daryl Eldridge (Nashville: Broadman & Holman, 1995), 299.
4. Paul D. Stanley and J. Robert Clinton, *Connecting: The Mentoring Relationships You Need to Succeed in Life* (Colorado Springs: NavPress, 1992), 33.

5. Richard Swenson, *Margin: Restoring Emotional, Physical, Financial, and Time Reserves to Overloaded Lives* (Colorado Springs: NavPress, 1992), 91-92.
6. Calvin Miller, *The Empowered Leader; 10 Keys to Servant Leadership* (Nashville: Broadman & Holman Publishers, 1995), 46.
7. Howard Hendricks, *Teaching to Change Lives* (Portland: Multnomah Press, 1987), 13.

Glossary

Affective—One of the major areas (domains) of aims that deals with influencing the feelings or emotions.

Aim—In education, the goal of the overall curriculum or an individual lesson. Aims deal with desired change in three primary areas (domains) of the student: knowing (cognitive domain), feeling (affective domain) and doing (volitional domain).

Behaviorism—Rooted in the psychological position that human beings are physical creatures and thus every aspect of human personality is essentially formed by a physical cause and effect process (or environmental influences). Educational behavioralists view learning as a mechanized process with specific outcomes observable in modified behavior. Alternative philosophies are developmentalism and relationalism.

Biblical Imperative—Something God, in His Word, has commanded to be done. For example, the Great Commission (Matthew 28:18-20; Acts 1:8) is a biblical imperative.

Cognitive—One of the major areas (domains) of aims that deals with helping a student to know something intellectually.

Curriculum—Literally "a racecourse," it refers to the plan of the entire educational process. Although it includes instructional materials, it is much more. It usually involves the development of a "scope and sequence" document (see below) and a philosophy of education.

Curriculum Materials—Refers to printed textbooks, leader's guides, and worksheets used in teaching a specific lesson or series of lessons. Also may include handcraft supplies, audio cassettes, videotapes, charts, posters, and any other physical items used in the teaching process.

Developmentalism—Rooted in the psychological position that growth patterns develop in the mental, physical, social, and moral growth of human beings. Educational developmentalists apply these patterns (cognitive-discovery approach) to creating curriculum plans best suited for students at their proper stage of development. Alternative philosophies are behaviorism and relationalism.

Hermeneutics—The study of the principles of interpreting the Bible.

Imago Dei—Latin phrase which refers to the fact that all human beings have been created in the image of God.

Learning Domains—The major divisions assigned to the way people learn. Usually divided as the cognitive, affective, and volitional (or psycho-motor) domains.

Lifechange—A coined phrase referring to the primary goal of Christian education; that is, change in students' lives as they mature in Christ.

Matrix—The arrangement of information into rows and columns to facilitate comprehension and application.

Modality—In education, it refers to the ways that students gather information using the senses. Thus, there is the auditory mode, the visual mode, the tactile/sensory mode.

Psycho-Motor—Action directly proceeding from mental activity.

Praxis—In general, it is the exercise of an art, science, or skill. In education, it usually refers to action informed by careful reflection.

Scope and Sequence—A document used in curriculum development containing the body of knowledge to be covered (the scope) and the order in which the subject will be taught (the sequence).

Serendipitous—In education, something which "just happens" in a teaching setting that has not specifically been planned. Sometimes referred to as a "teachable moment" or the "ah-hah!" experience.

Relationalism—The educational philosophy that relies on most mental growth taking place in relationship with other human beings. Evaluations place less emphasis on cognitive skills and developmental stages and more emphasis on the affective dimension of the learner. Spiritual development, therefore, places the teacher as facilitator for the self-directed learner.

Taxonomy—In general, the classification of any group of items. Educationally, it is used most often in reference to the classification of aims, such as in Bloom's *Taxonomy*.

Volitional—Often synonymous with psycho-motor, the emphasis rests on conduct response or action taken as a result of received information.

Bibliography

Chapter 1

Burgess, Howard. *Models of Religious Education: Theory and Practice in Historical and Contemporary Perspective.* Wheaton: Victor Books, 1996.

Eldridge, Daryl. *The Teaching Ministry of the Church.* Nashville: Broadman and Holman Publishers, 1996.

Hemphill, Ken. *Revitalizing the Sunday Morning Dinosaur.* Nashville: Broadman and Holman Publishers, 1996.

Hendricks, Howard, with Roberta Hestenes and Earl Palmer. *Mastering Teaching.* Portland: Multnomah Press, 1991.

Issler, Klaus, and Habermas, Ronald. *How We Learn: A Christian Teacher's Guide to Educational Psychology.* Grand Rapids: Baker Books, 1994.

Lebar, Lois E., with James E. Plueddemann. *Education That is Christian.* Wheaton: Victor Books, 1989.

Parkay, Forrest W., and Stanford, Beverly Hardcastle. *Becoming a Teacher,* 3rd ed. Needham Heights, MA: Allyn & Bacon, 1995.

Woolfolk, Anita F. *Educational Psychology,* 6th ed. Needham Heights, MA: Allyn & Bacon, 1995.

Yount, William R. *Created To Learn.* Nashville: Broadman and Holman Publishers, 1996.

Zuck, Roy B. *The Holy Spirit in Your Teaching.* Wheaton: Victor Books, 1963.

Chapter 2

Downs, Perry G. *Teaching for Spiritual Growth.* Grand Rapids: Zondervan Publishing House, 1994.

Gregory, John Milton. *The Laws of Teaching.* Grand Rapids: Baker Book House, 1954, 1975.

Pazmino, Robert W. *Principles and Practices of Christian Education.* Grand Rapids: Baker Books, 1992.

Wilhoit, James C., and Dettoni, John M. *Nurture That Is Christian; Developmental Perspectives on Christian Education.* Wheaton: Victor Books, 1995.

Willis, Wesley R. *Make Your Teaching Count.* Wheaton: Victor Books, 1985.

Chapter 3

Arthur, Kay. *How To Study Your Bible*. Eugene, OR: Harvest House Publishers, 1994.

Finzel, Hans. *Observe, Interpret, Apply: How to Study the Bible Inductively*. Wheaton: Victor Books, 1994.

Gangel, Kenneth O., and Hendricks, Howard G. *The Christian Educator's Handbook on Teaching*. Wheaton: Victor Books, 1988.

Haystead, Wes. *Bible 101*. Cincinnati: Standard Publishing Company, 1996.

Hendricks, Howard, and Hendricks, William D. *Living by the Book*. Chicago: Moody Press, 1991.

Jensen, Irving. *Enjoy Your Bible*. Wheaton: Harold Shaw Publishers, 1969, 1992.

Mears, Henrietta. *What the Bible Is All About*, revised. Ventura: Regal Books, 1997.

Powell, Terry. *You Can Lead a Bible Discussion Group!* Sisters, OR: Multnomah Books, 1996.

Sproul, R. C. *Knowing Scripture*. Downers Grove: InterVarsity Press, 1977.

Stein, Robert H. *A Basic Guide to Interpreting the Bible: Playing By the Rules*. Grand Rapids: Baker Books, 1994.

Wilhoit, Jim, and Ryken, Leland. *Effective Bible Teaching*. Grand Rapids: Baker Book House, 1988.

Chapter 4

Knowles, Malcom S. *The Modern Practice of Adult Education, From Pedagogy to Andragogy*. New York: Cambridge, 1980.

Kuhatschek, Jack. *Applying the Bible*. Grand Rapids: Zondervan Publishing Company, 1990.

McQuilkin, J. Robertson. *Understanding and Applying the Bible*. Chicago: Moody Press, 1983.

Richards, Lawrence O. *Creative Bible Teaching*. Chicago: Moody Press, 1970.

Schultz, Thom and Joani. *Why Nobody Learns Much of Anything at Church: And How to Fix it*. Loveland, CO: Group Publishing, 1993.

Veerman, Dave. *How to Apply the Bible*. Wheaton: Tyndale House Publishers, 1993.

Wilkinson, Bruce H. *The 7 Laws of the Learner*. Sisters, OR: Multnomah Press, 1992.

Chapter 5

Bloom, Benjamin S., et al. *Taxonomy of Educational Objectives. Handbook I: Cognitive Domain*. New York: David McKay, 1956.

Edge, Findley B. *Teaching For Results.* Nashville: Broadman and Holman Publishers, 1995.

Ford, LeRoy. *Design for Teaching and Training.* Nashville: Broadman Press, 1978.

Habermas, Ronald, and Issler, Klaus. *Teaching for Reconciliation.* Grand Rapids: Baker Book House, 1992.

Haystead, Wes. *The 21st Century Sunday School: Strategies for Today and Tomorrow.* Cincinnati: Standard Publishing Company, 1995.

Leypoldt, Martha M. *Learning Is Change, Adult Education in the Church.* Valley Forge: Judson Press, 1971.

Mager, Robert F., and Pipe, Peter. *Analyzing Performance Problems or 'You Really Oughta Wanna'.* Belmont, CA: Fearon Pitman Publishers, Inc., 1970.

Ortlund, Ray & Anne. *Renewal.* Colorado Springs: NavPress, 1989.

Tidwell, Charles A. *The Educational Ministry of a Church.* Nashville: Broadman and Holman, 1996.

Chapter 6

Briggs, Leslie J.; Gustafson, Kent L.; and Tillman, Murray H.; eds. *Instructional Design Principles and Applications,* 2nd ed. Englewood Cliffs, NJ: Educational Technology Publications, 1991.

Brown, Lowell E. *Sunday School Standards.* Ventura, CA: Gospel Light Publications, 1986.

Reiser, Robert A., and Dick, Walter. *Instructional Planning, A Guide for Teachers,* 2nd ed. Boston: Allyn and Bacon, 1996.

Tyler, Ralph. *Basic Principles of Curriculum and Instruction.* Chicago: University of Chicago Press.

Yelon, Stephen L. *Powerful Principles of Instruction.* White Plains, NY: Longman Publishing, 1996.

Chapter 8

Boulton, Barbara J., et al. *How to Do Bible Learning Activities,* Early Childhood I & II, Children I & II, Youth, and Adults. Ventura: Gospel Light Publications, 1982.

Bruce, Barbara. *7 Ways to Teach the Bible to Children.* Nashville: Abingdon Press, 1996.

Eggen, Paul D., and Kauchak, Donald P. *Strategies of Teachers, Teaching Content and Thinking Skills.* Boston: Allyn and Bacon, 1996.

Gangel, Kenneth O. *24 Ways to Improve Your Teaching.* Wheaton: Victor Books, 1986.

Gardner, Howard. *Frames of Mind: The Theory of Multiple Intelligences.* New York: Basic Books, 1983.

Gillis, Marcia, Crowley, Patty, and Gillis, Don, eds. *High Impact Teaching: Effective Lesson Planning,* video and book. Fort Worth: Resources For Ministry, 1990.

LeFever, Marlene. *Creative Teaching Methods.* Colorado Springs: Cook Ministry Resources, 1985, 1996.

_____. *Learning Styles, Reaching Everyone God Gave You to Teach.* Colorado Springs: David C. Cook Publishing Company, 1995.

Leypoldt, Martha M. *Learning is Change, Adult Education in the Church.* Valley Forge: Judson Press, 1971, 1978.

Mehlis, Marjie. *To Teach a Teacher.* Elgin, IL: David C. Cook Publishing Company, 1978.

Welter, Paul. *How to Help a Friend.* Wheaton: Tyndale House Publishers, 1978.

Chapter 10

Pierson, Jim, and Korth, Robert E., eds. *Special People, A Resource from Ministry with Persons Who Have Disabilities.* Cincinnati: Standard Publishing, 1989.

Chapter 11

Cangelosi, James S. *Evaluating Classroom Instruction.* New York: Longman, 1991.

Patterson, Richard. *Evaluating Church Education,* audio tapes. Wheaton: Evangelical Training Association, 1990.

Chapter 12

Hendricks, Howard. *Teaching to Change Lives.* Portland: Multnomah Press, 1987.

Miller, Calvin. *The Empowered Leader; 10 Keys to Servant Leadership.* Nashville: Broadman & Holman Publishers, 1995.

Stanley, Paul D., and Clinton, J. Robert. *Connecting: The Mentoring Relationships You Need to Succeed in Life.* Colorado Springs: NavPress, 1992.

Swenson, Richard. *Margin: Restoring Emotional, Physical, Financial, and Time Reserves to Overloaded Lives.* Colorado Springs: NavPress, 1992.

Trotman, Dawson. *Born to Reproduce.* Lincoln, NE: Back to the Bible Broadcast, 1975.